THE
WOMAN
IN ME

THE
WOMAN
IN ME

BRITNEY SPEARS

GALLERY BOOKS UK

First published in the United States by Gallery Books,
an imprint of Simon & Schuster LLC, 2023
First published in Great Britain by Gallery Books,
an imprint of Simon & Schuster UK Ltd, 2023

This edition published in Great Britain by Gallery Books,
an imprint of Simon & Schuster UK Ltd, 2024

1 3 5 7 9 10 8 6 4 2

Simon & Schuster UK Ltd
1st Floor
222 Gray's Inn Road
London WC1X 8HB

Simon & Schuster: Celebrating 100 Years of Publishing in 2024

www.simonandschuster.co.uk
www.simonandschuster.com.au
www.simonandschuster.co.in

Simon & Schuster Australia, Sydney
Simon & Schuster India, New Delhi

A CIP catalogue record for this book
is available from the British Library

Paperback ISBN: 978-1-3985-2254-1
eBook ISBN: 978-1-3985-2253-4

Interior design by Jaime Putorti

Printed and Bound in the UK using 100% Renewable
Electricity at CPI Group (UK) Ltd

For my boys, who are the loves of my life

THE
WOMAN
IN ME

PROLOGUE

As a little girl I walked for hours alone in the silent woods behind my house in Louisiana, singing songs. Being outside gave
me a sense of aliveness and danger. When I was growing up, my
mother and father fought constantly. He was an alcoholic. I was
usually scared in my home. Outside wasn't necessarily heaven,
either, but it was my world. Call it heaven or hell, it was mine.

Before going home, I would follow a path to our neighbors' house, through a landscaped yard and past a swimming
pool. They had a rock garden full of small, soft pebbles that
would trap the heat and stay warm in a way that felt so good
against my skin. I would lie down on those rocks and look up
at the sky, feeling the warmth from below and above, thinking:
I can make my own way in life. I can make my dreams come true.

Lying quietly on those rocks, I felt God.

1

Raising kids in the South used to be more about respecting your parents and keeping your mouth shut. (Today, the rules have reversed—it's more about respecting the kids.) Disagreeing with a parent was never permitted in my house. No matter how bad it got, there was an understanding to stay mute, and if I didn't, there were consequences.

In the Bible it says your tongue is your sword.

My tongue and my sword were me singing.

My whole childhood, I sang. I sang along with the car radio on the way to dance class. I sang when I was sad. To me, singing was spiritual.

I was born and went to school in McComb, Mississippi, and lived in Kentwood, Louisiana, twenty-five miles away.

Everyone knew everyone in Kentwood. Doors were left unlocked, social lives revolved around church and backyard parties, kids were put in matching outfits, and everyone knew how to shoot a gun. The area's main historic site was Camp Moore, a Confederate training base built by Jefferson Davis. Each year there are Civil War reenactments the weekend before Thanksgiving, and the sight of the people dressed up in military outfits was a reminder that the holiday was coming. I loved that time of year: hot chocolate, the smell of the fireplace in our living room, the colors of the fall leaves on the ground.

We had a little brick house with green-striped wallpaper and wood paneling. As a girl I went to Sonic, rode go-karts, played basketball, and attended a Christian school called Parklane Academy.

The first time I was truly touched and got shivers down my spine was hearing our housekeeper singing in the laundry room. I always did the family laundry and ironing, but when times were better financially, my mom would hire someone to help. The housekeeper sang gospel music, and it was literally an awakening to a whole new world. I'll never forget it.

Ever since then, my longing and passion to sing have grown. Singing is magic. When I sing, I own who I am. I can communicate purely. When you sing you stop using the language of "Hi, how are you . . ." You're able to say things that are much more profound. Singing takes me to a mystical place where language doesn't matter anymore, where anything is possible.

All I wanted was to be taken away from the everyday world

and into that realm where I could express myself without thinking. When I was alone with my thoughts, my mind filled with worries and fears. Music stopped the noise, made me feel confident, and took me to a pure place of expressing myself exactly as I wanted to be seen and heard. Singing took me into the presence of the divine. As long as I was singing, I was half outside the world. I'd be playing in the backyard like any kid would, but my thoughts and feelings and hopes were somewhere else.

I worked hard to make things look the way I wanted them to. I took myself very seriously when I shot silly music videos to Mariah Carey songs in my girlfriend's backyard. By age eight, I thought I was a director. Nobody in my town seemed to be doing stuff like that. But I knew what I wanted to see in the world, and I tried to make it so.

Artists make things and play characters because they want an escape into faraway worlds, and escape was exactly what I needed. I wanted to live inside my dreams, my wonderful fictitious world, and never think about reality if I could help it. Singing bridged reality and fantasy, the world I was living in and the world that I desperately wanted to inhabit.

Tragedy runs in my family. My middle name comes from my father's mother, Emma Jean Spears, who went by Jean. I've seen pictures of her, and I understand why everyone said we look alike. Same blond hair. Same smile. She looked younger than she was.

Her husband—my grandfather June Spears Sr.—was abusive. Jean suffered the loss of a baby when he was only three days old. June sent Jean to Southeast Louisiana Hospital, a by-all-accounts horrible asylum in Mandeville, where she was put on lithium. In 1966, when she was thirty-one, my grandmother Jean shot herself with a shotgun on her infant son's grave, just over eight years after his death. I can't imagine the grief that she must have felt.

The way people talk about men like June in the South is to say "Nothing was good enough for him," that he was "a perfectionist," that he was "a very involved father." I would probably put it more harshly than that.

A sports fanatic, June made my father exercise long past exhaustion. Each day when my father finished basketball practice, no matter how tired and hungry he was, he still had to shoot a hundred more baskets before he could come inside.

June was an officer for the Baton Rouge Police Department and he eventually had ten children with three wives. And as far as I can tell, no one has one good word to say about the first fifty years of his life. Even in my family, it was said that the Spears men tended to be bad news, especially in terms of how they treated women.

Jean wasn't the only wife June sent to the mental hospital in Mandeville. He sent his second wife there, too. One of my father's half sisters has said that June sexually abused her starting when she was eleven, until she ran away at sixteen.

My father was thirteen when Jean died on that grave. I know that trauma is part of why my father was how he was with my siblings and me; why, for him, nothing was ever good enough. My father pushed my brother to excel in sports. He drank until he couldn't think anymore. He'd disappear for days at a time. When my father drank, he was extremely mean.

But June softened as he got older. I didn't experience the vicious man who had abused my father and his siblings but rather a grandfather who seemed patient and sweet.

My father's world and my mother's world were completely opposite from each other.

According to my mother, my mom's mom—my grandmother Lilian "Lily" Portell—was from an elegant, sophisticated family in London. She had an exotic air about her that everyone commented on; her mother was British and her father was from the Mediterranean island of Malta. Her uncle was a bookbinder. The whole family played instruments and loved to sing.

During World War II, Lily met an American soldier, my grandfather Barney Bridges, at a dance for the soldiers. He was a driver for the generals and he loved driving fast.

She was disappointed, though, when he brought her with

him to America. She'd imagined a life like what she had in London. As she rode to his dairy farm from New Orleans, she looked out the window of Barney's car and was troubled by how empty his world seemed. "Where are all the lights?" she kept asking her new husband.

I sometimes think about Lily riding through the Louisiana countryside, looking out into the night, realizing that her large, vibrant, music-filled life of afternoon teas and London museums was about to become small and hard. Instead of going to the theater or shopping for clothes, she would have to spend her life cooped up in the country, cooking and cleaning and milking cows.

So my grandmother kept to herself, read a ton of books, became obsessed with cleaning, and missed London until the day she died. My family said that Barney didn't want to let Lily go back to London because he thought that if she went, she wouldn't come home.

My mother said Lily was so distracted by her own thoughts that she had a tendency to start clearing the table before everyone was done eating.

All I knew was that my grandmother was beautiful and I loved copying her British accent. Talking in a British accent has always made me happy because it makes me think of her, my fashionable grandmother. I wanted to have manners and a lilting voice just like hers.

Because Lily had money, my mother, Lynne; her brother,

Sonny; and her sister, Sandra, grew up with what you might consider money-money, especially for rural Louisiana. Even though they were Protestant, my mom attended Catholic school. She was gorgeous as a teenager, with her black hair worn short. She'd always go to school wearing the highest boots and the tiniest skirts. She hung out with the gay guys in town, who gave her rides on their motorcycles.

My father took an interest in her, as well he might. And probably in part because June made him work so ridiculously hard, my father was unbelievably talented at sports. People would drive for miles just to see him play basketball.

My mom saw him and she said, "Oh, who is this?"

By all accounts, their relationship was born of mutual attraction and a sense of adventure. But the honeymoon was over long before I came along.

2

When they got married, my parents lived in a small home in Kentwood. My mother was no longer supported by her family, so my parents were very poor. They were young, too— my mom was twenty-one and my father was twenty-three. In 1977, they had my big brother, Bryan. When they left that first small place, they bought a little three-bedroom ranch house.

After Bryan was born, my mom went back to school to become a teacher. My dad, who worked as a welder at oil refineries—hard jobs that would last a month or sometimes three—started to drink heavily, and before too long, that was taking its toll on the family. The way my mom tells it, a couple of years into the marriage, my grandfather Barney, my mom's dad, died in a car accident, and in the aftermath, my dad went on a bender, missing Bryan's first birthday party. When Bryan was a toddler, my father got drunk at a Christmas party and

11

went AWOL on Christmas morning. That time my mother said she'd had enough. She went to stay with Lily. That March of 1980, she filed for divorce. But June and June's new wife begged her to take him back, and she did.

For a while, apparently, everything was calm. My dad stopped welding and started a construction business. Then, after a lot of struggle, he got a gym business going, too. It was called Total Fitness and it transformed some of the men in town, including my uncles, into bodybuilders. He ran it in a detached studio space on our property, next door to the house. An endless string of muscular men streamed in and out of the gym, flexing their muscles in the mirrors under the fluorescent lights.

My dad started doing really well. In our little town he became one of the most well-off men. My family threw big backyard crawfish boils. They had crazy parties, with dancing all night long. (I've always assumed their secret ingredient for staying up all night was speed, since that was the drug of choice back then.)

My mom opened a daycare center with her sister, my aunt Sandra. To cement their marriage, my parents had a second baby—me. I was born on December 2, 1981. My mother never missed an opportunity to recall that she was in excruciating labor with me for twenty-one hours.

* * *

I loved the women in my family. My aunt Sandra, who already had two sons, had a surprise baby at thirty-five: my cousin Laura Lynne. Just a few months apart, Laura Lynne and I were like twins, and we were best friends. Laura Lynne was always like a sister to me, and Sandra was a second mother. She was so proud of me and so encouraging.

And even though my grandmother Jean was gone long before I was born, I was lucky enough to know her mother, my great-grandmother Lexie Pierce. Lexie was *wicked* beautiful, always made up with a white, white face and red, red lipstick. She was a badass, more and more so as she got older. I was told, and had no trouble believing, that she'd been married seven times. Seven! Obviously, she disliked her son-in-law June, but after her daughter Jean died, she stuck around and took care of my father and his siblings, and then her great-grandchildren, too.

Lexie and I were very close. My most vivid and joyful memories of being a little girl are of times spent with her. We'd have sleepovers, just the two of us. At night, we'd go through her makeup cabinet. In the morning, she would make me a huge breakfast. Her best friend, who lived next door, would come over to visit and we'd listen to slow 1950s ballads from Lexie's record collection. During the day, Lexie and I would nap together. I loved nothing more than drifting off to sleep by her side, smelling her face powder and her perfume, listening as her breathing grew deep and regular.

One day, Lexie and I went to rent a movie. As we drove away from the video rental place, she ran into another car, then got stuck in a hole. We couldn't get out. A tow truck had to come rescue us. That accident scared my mother. From then on, I wasn't allowed to hang out with my great-grandmother.

"It wasn't even a bad accident!" I told my mother. I begged to see Lexie. She was my favorite person.

"No, I'm afraid she's getting senile," my mom said. "It's not safe for you to be with her alone anymore."

After that, I saw her at my house, but I couldn't get in the car with her or have sleepovers with her ever again. It was a huge loss for me. I didn't understand how being with someone I loved could be considered dangerous.

At that age, my favorite thing to do besides spending time with Lexie was hiding in cabinets. It became a family joke: "Where's Britney now?" At my aunt's house, I always disappeared. Everyone would mount a search for me. Just when they'd start to panic, they'd open a cabinet door and there I'd be.

I must have wanted them to look for me. For years that was my thing—to hide.

Hiding was one way I got attention. I also loved dancing and singing. I sang in the choir of our church, and I took dance classes three nights a week and on Saturdays. Then I added gymnastics classes an hour away in Covington, Louisiana. When it came to dancing and singing and acrobatics, I couldn't get enough.

At career day in elementary school, I said I was going to be a lawyer, but neighbors and teachers started to say that I was "Broadway bound," and eventually I embraced my identity as "the little entertainer."

I was three at my first dance recital and four when I sang my first solo: "What Child Is This?" for a Christmas program at my mother's daycare.

I wanted to hide, but I also wanted to be seen. Both things could be true. Crouched in the cool darkness of a cabinet, I felt so small I could disappear. But with everyone's eyes on me, I became something else, someone who could command a room. In white tights, belting out a song, I felt like anything was possible.

3

"Ms. Lynne! Ms. Lynne!" the boy shouted. He was out of breath, panting at our front door. "You have to come! Come now!"

One day when I was four, I was in the living room of our house, sitting on the couch with my mom on one side and my friend Cindy on the other. Kentwood was like a town in a soap opera—there was *always* drama. Cindy was chattering away to my mom about the latest scandal while I was listening in, trying to follow along, when the door burst open. The boy's facial expression was enough for me to know something terrifying had happened. My heart dropped.

My mother and I started running. The road had just been repaved and I was barefoot, running on the hot black tar.

"Ow! Ow! Ow!" I yelped with every step. I looked down at my feet and saw the tar sticking to them.

Finally, we arrived at the field where my brother, Bryan, had been playing with his neighbor friends. They had been trying to mow down some tall grass with their four-wheelers. This seemed like a fantastic idea to them because they were idiots. Inevitably, they couldn't see one another through the tall grass and had a head-on collision.

I must have seen everything, heard Bryan hollering in pain, my mother screaming in fear, but I don't remember any of it. I think God made me black out so I wouldn't remember the pain and panic, or the sight of my brother's crushed body.

A helicopter airlifted him to the hospital.

When I visited Bryan days later, he was in a full body cast. From what I could see, he'd broken nearly every bone in his body. And the detail that drove it all home for me, as a kid, was that he had to pee through a hole in the cast.

The other thing I couldn't help but notice was that the whole room was full of toys. My parents were so grateful he'd survived and they felt so bad for him that during his recovery, every day was Christmas. My mom catered to my brother because of guilt. She still defers to him to this day. It's funny how one split second can change a family's dynamics forever.

The accident made me much closer to my brother. Our bond was formed out of my sincere, genuine recognition of his pain. Once he came home from the hospital, I wouldn't leave his side. I slept beside him every night. He couldn't sleep in his own bed because he still had the full body cast. So he had a special bed, and they had to set up a little mattress for me at the foot of it. Sometimes I'd climb into his bed and just hold him.

Once the cast came off, I continued to share a bed with him for years. Even as a very little girl, I knew that—between the accident and how hard our dad was on him—my brother had a difficult life. I wanted to bring him comfort.

Finally, after years of this, my mom told me, "Britney, now you're almost in the sixth grade. You need to start sleeping by yourself!"

I said no.

I was such a baby—I did not want to sleep by myself. But she insisted, and finally I had to give in.

Once I started to stay in my own room, I came to enjoy having my own space, but I remained extremely close to my brother. He loved me. And I loved him so much—for him I felt the most endearing, protective love. I didn't want him ever to be hurt. I'd seen him suffer too much already.

As my brother got better, we became heavily involved with the community. Since it was a small town of just a couple thousand people, everyone came out to support the three main parades a year—Mardi Gras, Fourth of July, Christmas. The whole town looked forward to them. The streets would be lined with people smiling, waving, leaving behind the drama of their lives for a day to have fun watching their neighbors slowly wander by on Highway 38.

One year, a bunch of us kids decided to decorate a golf cart and put it in the Mardi Gras parade. There were probably eight kids in that golf cart—way too many, obviously. There were three on the bench seat, a couple standing on the sides holding on to the little roof, and one or two swinging from the back. It was so heavy that the tires of the cart were almost flat. We all wore nineteenth-century costumes; I can't even remember why. I was sitting on the laps of the bigger kids up front, waving at everyone. The problem was, with that many kids in a golf cart, and its flat tires, the thing got hard to control, and with the laughing and the waving and the excited energy . . . Well, we only hit the car ahead of us a *few* times, but that was enough for us to get expelled from the parade.

4

When my father started drinking heavily again, his businesses started to fail.

The stress of having no money was compounded by the chaos of my father's extreme mood swings. I was particularly scared to get in the car with my dad because he would talk to himself while he was driving. I couldn't understand the words he was saying. He seemed to be in his own world.

I knew even then that my father had reasons for wanting to lose himself in drinking. He was stressed out by work. Now I see even more clearly that he was self-medicating after enduring years of abuse at the hands of his father, June. At the time, though, I had no idea why he was so hard on us, why nothing we did seemed to be quite good enough for him.

The saddest part to me was that what I always wanted was a dad who would love me as I was—somebody who would say,

"I just love you. You could do anything right now. I'd still love you with unconditional love."

My dad was reckless, cold, and mean with me, but he was even harder on Bryan. He pushed him so hard to do well in sports that it was cruel. Bryan's life in those years was much rougher than mine because our father put him through the same brutal regimen June had pushed on him. Bryan was forced to do basketball and also football, even though he wasn't built for it.

My dad could also be abusive with my mom, but he was more the type of drinker who would go away for days at a time. To be honest, it was a kindness to us when he went away. I preferred it when he wasn't there.

What made his time at home especially bad was that my mom would argue with him all night long. He was so drunk he couldn't talk. I don't know if he could even hear her. But we could. Bryan and I had to suffer the consequences of her rage, which meant not being able to sleep through the night. Her screaming voice would echo through the house.

I'd storm out into the living room in my nightgown and beg her, "Just feed him and go put him to bed! He's sick!"

She was arguing with this person who wasn't even conscious. But she wouldn't listen. I would go back to bed furious, staring daggers at the ceiling, listening to her yell, cursing her in my heart.

Isn't that awful? He was the one who was drunk. He was the one whose alcoholism had made us so poor. He was the one passed out in the chair. But she was the one who ended up pissing me off the most, because at least in those moments, he was quiet. I was so desperate to sleep, and she wouldn't shut up.

In spite of all the nightly drama, by day my mom made our home a place my friends wanted to come to—at least when my father respected us enough to drink somewhere else. All the kids from the neighborhood came over. Our house was, for lack of a better word, the cool house. We had a high bar with twelve chairs around it. My mom was a typical young Southern mom, often gossiping, always smoking cigarettes with her friends at the bar (she smoked Virginia Slims, the same cigarettes I smoke now) or talking with them on the phone. I was dead to all of them. The older kids would sit on the bar chairs in front of the TV and play video games. I was the youngest one; I didn't know how to play video games, so I always had to fight to get the older kids' attention.

Our house was a zoo. I was always dancing on the coffee table for attention, and my mom was always chasing after Bryan when he was little, jumping over couches trying to catch him so she could spank him after back-talking her.

I was always overly excited, trying to draw the older kids' eyes away from the screen in the living room or to get the adults to stop talking to one another in the kitchen.

"Britney, stop!" my mother would yell. "We have company! Just be nice. Be on good behavior."

But I ignored her. And I would always find a way to get everyone's attention.

5

I was quiet and small, but when I sang I came alive, and I had taken enough gymnastics classes to be able to move well. When I was five, I entered a local dance competition. My talent was a dance routine done wearing a top hat and twirling a cane. I won. Then my mother started taking me around to contests all over the region. In old photos and videos, I'm wearing the most ridiculous things. In my third-grade musical, I wore a baggy purple T-shirt with a huge purple bow on top of my head that made me look like a Christmas present. It was absolutely horrible.

I worked my way through the talent circuit, winning a regional contest in Baton Rouge. Before too long, my parents set their sights on bigger opportunities than what we could accomplish picking up prizes in school gymnasiums. When they saw an advertisement in the newspaper for an open call for *The*

All New Mickey Mouse Club, they suggested we go. We drove eight hours to Atlanta. There were more than two thousand kids there. I had to stand out—especially once we learned, after we arrived, that they were only looking for kids over the age of ten.

When the casting director, a man named Matt Casella, asked me how old I was, I opened my mouth to say "Eight," then remembered the age-ten cutoff and said: "Nine!" He looked at me skeptically.

For my audition, I sang "Sweet Georgia Brown" while doing a dance routine, adding in some gymnastics flips.

They narrowed the group of thousands from across the country down to a handful of kids, including a beautiful girl from California a few years older than me named Keri Russell.

A girl from Pennsylvania named Christina Aguilera and I were told we hadn't made the cut but that we were talented. Matt said we could probably get on the show once we were a little older and more experienced. He told my mom that he thought we should go to New York City to work. He recommended we look up an agent he liked who helped young performers get started in the theater.

We didn't go right away. Instead, for about six months, I stayed in Louisiana, and I went to work, waiting tables at Lexie's seafood restaurant, Granny's Seafood and Deli, to help out.

The restaurant had a terrible, fishy smell. Still, the food was amazing—unbelievably good. And it became the new hangout for all the kids. The deli's back room was where my brother and all his friends would get drunk in high school. Meanwhile, out on the floor, at age nine, I was cleaning shellfish and serving plates of food while doing my prissy dancing in my cute little outfits.

My mom sent footage of me to the agent Matt had recommended, Nancy Carson. In the video, I was singing "Shine On, Harvest Moon." It worked: she asked us to come to New York and meet with her.

After I sang for Nancy in her office twenty stories up in a building in Midtown Manhattan, we got back on the Amtrak and headed home. I had been officially signed by a talent agency.

Not long after we got back to Louisiana, my little sister, Jamie Lynn, was born. Laura Lynne and I spent hours playing with her in the playhouse like she was another one of our dolls.

A few days after she came home with the baby, I was getting ready for a dance competition when my mother started acting strangely. She was hand-sewing a rip in my costume, but while working the needle and thread she just up and threw the costume away. She didn't seem to know what she was doing. The costume was a piece of shit, frankly, but I needed it to compete.

"Mama! Why did you throw my costume away?" I said.

Then all of a sudden there was blood. Blood *everywhere*.

Something hadn't been sewn up properly after she gave birth. She was gushing blood. I screamed for my father. "What's wrong with her?" I yelled. "What's wrong with her?"

Daddy rushed in and drove her to the hospital. The whole way, I kept screaming, "Something cannot be wrong with my mom!"

I was nine. To see a river of blood flowing out of your mother would be traumatic for anyone, but for a child at that age, it was terrifying. I had never seen that much blood before.

Once we got to the doctor, they fixed her in what felt to me like two seconds. No one even seemed that concerned. Apparently, postpartum hemorrhage isn't that uncommon. But it lodged in my memory.

At gymnastics class, I'd always check to make sure my mom was on the other side of the window, waiting for me to be done. It was a reflex, something I had to do to feel safe. But one day I did my usual check-in out the window and she wasn't there. I panicked. She'd left. She was gone! Maybe forever! I started crying. I fell to my knees. Seeing me, you'd have thought someone had just died.

My teacher rushed over to comfort me. "Honey, she's going to come back!" she said. "It's okay! She probably just went to Walmart!"

It turned out that my mom had done exactly that: she had gone to Walmart. But it was not okay. I couldn't take her leaving. Seeing how upset I was when she got back, she never left that window during class again. And for the next few years she never left my side.

I was a little girl with big dreams. I wanted to be a star like Madonna, Dolly Parton, or Whitney Houston. I had simpler dreams, too, dreams that seemed even harder to achieve and that felt too ambitious to say out loud: *I want my dad to stop drinking. I want my mom to stop yelling. I want everyone to be okay.*

With my family, anything could go wrong at any time. I had no power there. Only while performing was I truly invincible. Standing in a Manhattan conference room in front of a woman who could make my dreams come true, at least one thing was completely within my control.

6

When I was ten, I was invited to be a contestant on *Star Search*.

On the first show, I did a spunky version of a song I'd heard sung by Judy Garland: "I Don't Care." I got 3.75 stars. My rival, a girl who sang opera, got 3.5. I advanced to the next round. The next episode taped later that day, and I was up against a bolo-tie-wearing boy with a lot of hair spray in his hair named Marty Thomas, age twelve. We were friendly; we even played basketball together before the show. I sang the Judds' "Love Can Build a Bridge," which I'd sung the year before at my aunt's wedding.

While we were waiting for our scores, Marty and I were interviewed onstage by the host, Ed McMahon.

"I noticed last week, you have the most adorable, pretty eyes," he said to me. "Do you have a boyfriend?"

"No, sir," I said.

"Why not?"

"They're mean."

"Boyfriends?" Ed said. "You mean all boys are mean? I'm not mean! How about me?"

"Well, it depends," I said.

"I get that a lot," Ed said.

I got 3.75 again. Marty got a perfect 4. I smiled and hugged him politely, and as I walked off, Ed wished me luck. I kept it together until I made it backstage—but then I burst into tears. Afterward, my mom got me a hot fudge sundae.

My mom and I kept flying back and forth to New York. The intensity of working in the city as a little girl was exciting for me, even if it was also intimidating.

I got offered a job: an understudy role in the off-Broadway musical *Ruthless!*, inspired by *The Bad Seed*, *All About Eve*, *Mame*, and *Gypsy*. I played a sociopathic child star named Tina Denmark. Tina's first song was called "Born to Entertain." It hit close to home. The other understudy was a talented young actress named Natalie Portman.

While I was doing the show, we rented a little apartment for my mom, baby Jamie Lynn, and me near my public school, the Professional Performing Arts School, and I took classes nearby at Broadway Dance Center. But mostly I passed my time at the Players Theatre downtown.

The experience was a validation in some way, proof I had enough talent to make it in the theatrical world. But it was a grueling schedule. There was no time to be a regular kid or really make friends, because I had to work nearly every day. On Saturdays there were two shows.

I also didn't love being an understudy. I had to be at the theater every night until as late as midnight, in case I had to take over for the main Tina, Laura Bell Bundy. After a few months, she left and I took over the lead, but I was awfully worn out.

By the time Christmas came around, I desperately wanted to go home—and then I learned I was supposed to perform on Christmas Day. In tears, I asked my mom, "Am I really going to do this for *Christmas?*" I looked at the little mini tree in our apartment, thinking about the sturdy evergreen we'd have in our living room in Kentwood.

In my little-girl mind, I didn't understand why I'd want to do that—continue performing through the holidays. So I quit the show and went home.

The schedule of New York City theater was just too rough on me at that age. One good thing did come out of it, though: I learned how to sing in a theater with small acoustics. The audience is right beside you—just two hundred people in the room. Honestly, it's strange, but in that space, the feeling of singing is more electric. The closeness that you feel with the people in the audience is something special. Their energy made me stronger.

With that experience under my belt, I auditioned again for the *Mickey Mouse Club*.

Waiting to hear about the *Mickey Mouse Club* back in Kentwood, attending Parklane Academy, I became a basketball point guard. I was tiny for eleven, but I could run the plays. People imagine I was a cheerleader, but I never was. I danced a little bit on the side, but at school I wanted to play ball, so I did in spite of my height. I had this huge number 25 jersey, way too big for me. I was a little bitty mouse zipping around out there.

I had a crush for a while on a basketball player who was fifteen or sixteen. He made every three-pointer, and he made it look easy. People would come from far away to see him play, just like they had to see my dad. He was good—not as good as my dad had been, but still, a genius with the ball.

I marveled at him and my friends who were taller than me. My thing was to steal the ball away from an opposing player mid-dribble, run down, and make a layup.

I loved the thrill of quickly weaving around the other team. Just the rush of no script, the play being unpredictable, completely unknown, made me feel so alive. I was so small and so sweet that no one saw me coming.

It wasn't the same as being onstage in New York City—but under the bright lights on the court, waiting for the sound of applause, it felt like the next best thing.

7

My second audition for the *Mickey Mouse Club* got me booked. Matt, the nice casting director who had referred my mom to our agent, Nancy, decided I was ready.

Being in the show was boot camp for the entertainment industry: there were extensive dance rehearsals, singing lessons, acting classes, time in the recording studio, and school in between. The Mouseketeers quickly split into our own cliques, divided by the dressing rooms that we shared: Christina Aguilera and I were the younger kids, and we shared a dressing room with another girl, Nikki DeLoach. We looked up to the older kids—Keri Russell, Ryan Gosling, and Tony Lucca, who I thought was so handsome. And quickly I connected with a boy named Justin Timberlake.

We were shooting at Disney World in Orlando, and my mom and Jamie Lynn, who at the time was two years old, had come along with me. During the day, for our breaks, the cast would go ride rides and goof off. It was honestly a kid's dream—unbelievably fun, particularly for a kid like me. But it was also exceptionally hard work: we would run choreography thirty times in a day, trying to get every step perfect.

The only bad moment was when, not long into filming, we got a call that my grandmother Lily had died. Maybe because of a heart attack or stroke, she drowned in the pool while swimming. We couldn't afford to fly home for the funeral, but Lynn Harless, Justin's kind mother, lent us the plane fare. It was something family would do, and the kids and parents on that show became family.

One day, Tony was looking for a hat that a wardrobe person had left in the girls' room, and he came into our dressing room. He walked in and my heart fell out of my chest. He was my crush. I couldn't believe the guy had just walked into my dressing room! My little heart just went to the floor.

Another time, at a sleepover, we played a game of Truth or Dare, and someone dared Justin to kiss me. A Janet Jackson song was playing in the background as he leaned in and kissed me.

It took me back to a moment in the library when I was in the third grade, holding a guy's hand for the first time. It was the biggest deal to me, so real, so powerful. That was the first time somebody had paid me any sort of romantic attention, and it felt like a wonderful rebellion. The lights were off—we'd been watching a movie, and we hid our hands underneath the desk so the teachers couldn't see.

The *Mickey Mouse Club* was a terrific experience; it got my feet wet in TV. Performing on that show *ignited* me. From then on I knew I wanted to do what I did there—singing and dancing.

When the show ended a year and a half later, a lot of my castmates were going off to New York or Los Angeles to continue chasing their dreams. But I decided to go back to Kentwood. Already within me was a push-pull: part of me wanted to keep building toward the dream; the other part wanted to live a normal life in Louisiana. For a minute, I had to let normalcy win.

Back at home, I returned to Parklane, settling into normal teenage life—or the closest thing to "normal" that was possible in my family.

For fun, starting when I was in eighth grade, my mom and I would make the two-hour drive from Kentwood to Biloxi, Mississippi, and while we were there, we would drink daiquiris. We called our cocktails "toddies." I loved that I was able to drink with my mom every now and then. The way we drank was nothing like how my father did it. When he drank, he grew more depressed and shut down. We became happier, more alive and adventurous.

Some of my best times with my mom were those trips we took to the beach with my sister. As we'd drive, I'd sip on a little bitty White Russian. To me, the drink tasted like ice cream. When it had the perfect amount of shaved ice and cream and sugar and not too much alcohol, that was my piece of heaven.

My sister and I had matching bathing suits and matching perms. Now, today it's basically illegal to give a little kid a perm, but back in the nineties it was just *cute as hell*. At three, Jamie Lynn was a living doll—the craziest, most adorable child ever.

So that was our thing. We'd go to Biloxi, drink, go to the beach, come back happy. And we had fun. We had a *lot* of fun. Even amid all the darkness, there was still a lot of joy in my childhood.

By thirteen, I was drinking with my mom and smoking with my friends. I had my first cigarette at my one "bad" friend's house. All my other friends were geeks, but this friend was popular: her sister was a senior and she always had the best makeup, and guys were all over her.

She took me out to a shed and handed me my first cigarette. Even though it was just tobacco, I felt *high*. I remember thinking, *Am I going to die? Is this feeling going to go away? When is this feeling going to go away?* Once I survived my first cigarette, I immediately wanted another one.

I did a pretty good job hiding my habit from my mother, but one day she was having me drive us home from the store along the long road that led to our house—I started driving at thirteen, too—when suddenly she started sniffing the air.

"I smell smoke!" she said. "Have you been smoking?"

She grabbed one of my hands off the wheel fast and pulled it to her to smell. As she did that, I lost control of the wheel, and the car spun off the road. It felt like everything was moving in slow motion. I looked back and saw little Jamie Lynn pressed backward into the seat: she had on a seat belt but wasn't in a car seat. As we spun what felt like very slowly, I kept thinking, *We're gonna die. We're gonna die. We're gonna die.*

Then, *wham!* The butt of the car hit a telephone pole.

Hitting the way we did was a miracle. If we'd hit the pole going forward, we would've gone through the windshield. My mother jumped out of the car and just started yelling—at me for crashing, at cars passing by for help, at the world for letting this happen.

No one was hurt, fortunately. All three of us walked away. Even better: my mom forgot all about how she'd caught me smoking. The crime of teenage me smoking? *Whatever. We almost died!* After that, she never mentioned it again.

*   *   *

One day some of the boys in the sixth grade at school asked me to go smoke a cigarette in their locker room during break. I was the only girl they ever asked to join them. I've never felt cooler. Fortunately, the boys' locker room had two doors, one of which led to the outside. I remember we jammed the door open so the smoke could escape and we wouldn't get caught.

It became a ritual. But it didn't last. A little while later, I decided to try it on my own, without the boys. This time my best girlfriend and I went to smoke in the girls' locker room, but that room only had one door. Disaster—we got caught red-handed and were sent to the principal's office.

"Were you smoking?" the principal asked.

"No!" I said. My best friend reached down and secretly pinched my hand so hard. It was clear the principal didn't believe me, but guess what—somehow we actually got away with just a warning.

Later my friend said, "I swear to God, Britney, you're the worst liar I've ever seen in my life. Let me do the talking next time, please."

I wasn't just drinking and smoking by that age; I was precocious when it came to boys. I had a huge crush on one of the guys who was always hanging around my "bad" friend's house. He was eighteen or nineteen, and he had a girlfriend at the time—a tomboy. They were really together, the "it" couple at our school. I wished he'd look at me, but I didn't have much hope given that I was five years younger than him.

One night, I was sleeping over at my "bad" friend's house. With no warning, the guy I had a crush on snuck into the house in the middle of the night—it must have been three in the morning. I was sleeping on the couch, and I woke up to him sitting next to me. He started kissing me, and then we were fully making out on the couch.

What is happening? I thought. It was like some sort of séance—like I'd conjured him! I couldn't believe my crush had just appeared out of nowhere and started making out with me. And it was sweet. That was all he did—kiss me. He didn't try anything else.

That year I liked a lot of the boys in my brother's crowd. As a kid, Bryan was funny—*weird*, in the best way. But when he was a senior, he became king of the school, an absolute badass.

His senior year, I started dating his best friend, and I lost my virginity to him.

I was young for the ninth grade, and the guy was seventeen. My relationship with him ended up consuming a lot of my time. I would go to school like normal at seven a.m. but leave at lunchtime, around one p.m., and spend the afternoon with him. Then he would drive me back right as school was getting out. I'd just innocently get on the bus and go home like nothing had happened.

Eventually, my mom got a call from the school office; I'd missed seventeen days, which I had to make up.

My mom said, "How did you do it? How did you just leave?"

"Oh, I forged your signature," I said.

The age difference between me and that guy was huge, obviously—now it seems outrageous—and so my brother, who was always very protective, started to hate him. When Bryan caught me sneaking out to go visit his friend, he told on me to our parents. As punishment, I had to walk around the neighborhood all day with a bucket, cleaning up garbage like a prisoner on the highway. Bryan followed me around taking pictures as, crying, I picked up trash.

Moments like that aside, there was something so beautifully normal about that period of my life: going to homecoming and prom, driving around our little town, going to the movies.

But, the truth was, I missed performing. My mom had been in touch with a lawyer she'd met on my audition circuit, a man named Larry Rudolph, who she would call sometimes for business advice. She sent him videos of me singing, and he suggested I record a demo. He had a song that Toni Braxton had recorded for her second album that had ended up on the cutting-room floor; it was called "Today." He sent me the song and I learned it, then I recorded it at a studio an hour and a half away from us, in New Orleans. This would become the demo that I would use to get in the door at record labels.

Around the same time, Justin and another Mouseketeer, JC Chasez, were in a new boy band called NSYNC that was being assembled. Another castmate, Nikki, with whom I'd shared that dressing room, was joining a girl group, but after I talked it over with my mom, we decided to pursue the solo avenue instead.

Larry played the demo for some executives in New York who told him they wanted to see what I could do. So I put on my little-bitty heels and my cute little dress, and I returned to New York.

I had tried to go back to being an ordinary teenager, but it hadn't worked. I still wanted something more.

...Downloaded Five Records, maybe

8

Who is this man? I thought. *I have no idea, but I like his office, and I really like his dog.* He was just this little old man, but his energy was insane. I estimated that he was probably sixty-five years old (he was actually in his fifties).

Larry had told me the man was a big contact named Clive Calder. I had no idea what he did. If I'd known going in that he was a record executive who'd founded Jive Records, maybe I would have been more nervous. Instead, I was just curious. And I loved him from the second I met him.

He had an incredibly intimidating three-story office. And in the office was a teacup terrier—a kind of dog I didn't even know existed—that was, I swear to God, the smallest, most precious thing. When I walked in and saw that office and that dog, I felt like I was entering a parallel universe. Everything opened up into a different dimension. I walked into an amazing dream.

"Hi, Britney!" he said, practically vibrating with enthusiasm. "How are ya?"

He acted like he was part of some sort of powerful secret society. He had a South African accent that made it sound to me like he was a character in an old movie. I'd never heard anyone talk that way in real life.

He let me pick up his dog. As I held the tiny animal, so warm in my arms, and looked around at the giant office, I couldn't stop smiling. In that moment, my dreams got a jump start.

I hadn't recorded anything yet other than the demo. I was just visiting these people Larry had told me to meet with. I knew I was supposed to go sing a song for record label executives. And I knew I sure wanted to be around that guy more, and that the way he was had something to do with the way I wanted to be. I wouldn't have been surprised if he'd been my uncle in a past life. I wanted to always know him.

It was his smile. Clever, smart, wise. He was a mystical smile of a man. I'll never forget it. I felt so much joy with him, and I felt like the trip to New York was more than worthwhile even if all it gave me was the chance to meet someone like that, someone who believed in me.

But my day wasn't done. Larry took me around town, and I went into rooms full of executives and sang Whitney Houston's "I Have Nothing." Gazing out at rooms full of men in suits looking me up and down in my small dress and high heels, I sang *loud*.

Clive signed me right away. And so I ended up getting a recording deal with Jive Records at the age of fifteen.

My mother was teaching second grade now in Kentwood, and Jamie Lynn was little, so we got our family friend Felicia Culotta (I called her "Miss Fe") to come with me everywhere.

The label wanted me in a studio immediately. They put Fe and me up in an apartment in New York. We would drive to New Jersey every day and I would go into a booth and sing for producer and songwriter Eric Foster White, who'd worked with Whitney Houston.

Honestly, I was clueless. I didn't know what was going on. I just knew I loved to sing and I loved to dance, and so whichever of the gods could come down and coordinate that for me, I was going to show up for them. If anyone was able to put something together for me that presented me in a format people could relate to, I was ready. I don't know what happened, but God worked his magic, and there I was in New Jersey, recording.

The booth I sang in was underground. When you're inside it, you just hear yourself sing, nothing else. I did that for months. I never came out of the booth.

After working nonstop, I went to a barbecue at someone's house. I was very girly at the time—always in a dress and heels. I was there talking with people, trying to make a good impression, and at one point I ran to go get Felicia and bring her out on the balcony. I didn't realize that there was a screen door there. I ran straight into it, hit it with my nose, and fell back. Everyone looked up and saw me on the floor, holding my nose.

When I tell you I was embarrassed, I swear to *God* . . .

I got up and someone said, "You know there's a screen there."

"Yeah, thanks," I said.

Of course, everyone just laughed their little fannies off.

I was *so* embarrassed. Isn't it funny that out of all the things that happened to me in that first year of recording, that is one of my most vivid memories? That was over twenty-five years ago! I was devastated! But honestly, I think I was more in shock because I did not know that screen was there. It made me think I might have been recording in that booth for too long.

About a year into my time in New Jersey, things were coming together for my first album. Then all of a sudden one of the executives told me, "You need to meet this producer from Sweden. He's really good. He writes cool songs."

"All right," I said. "Who has he worked with?"

I don't know how I knew to ask that question, inexperienced as I was, but I'd started to have clear ideas about how I wanted to sound. I did a little bit of research, too, and learned that at that point he'd done songs for the Backstreet Boys, Robyn, and Bryan Adams.

"Yes," I said. "Let's do it."

Max Martin flew to New York and we had a dinner meeting, just me and him, with no assistants or label people. Even though I usually had handlers around because of my age, in this case they wanted me to meet him by myself. As we sat down, a waiter came over and said, "How may I help you?"

Somehow a candle flipped over and sent the whole table up in flames.

We were at one of the most expensive restaurants in New York City, and our table had just become a wall of fire—from "How may I help you?" to flame wall in under a second.

Max and I looked at each other in horror. "We should go now, yeah?" he said.

He was magic. And we started working together.

I flew to Sweden to record songs, but I barely registered the difference between there and New Jersey: I was just in another booth.

Felicia would come in and say, "Do you want some coffee? Let's go take a break!"

I would shake her off. I worked for hours straight. My work ethic was strong. I would never come out. If you knew me then, you wouldn't hear from me for days. I would stay in the studio as long as I could. If anyone wanted to leave, I'd say, "I wasn't perfect."

The night before we recorded ". . . Baby One More Time," I was listening to Soft Cell's "Tainted Love" and fell in love with that sound. I stayed up late so that I'd go into the studio tired, my voice fried. It worked. When I sang, it came out gravelly in a way that sounded more mature and sexier.

Once I felt what was happening, I became so focused on the recording. And Max listened to me. When I said I wanted more R&B in my voice, less straight pop, he knew what I meant and he made it happen.

Then, when all the songs were done, someone said, "What else can you do? Do you want to dance now?"

I said, "Do I want to dance? Hell yeah, I do!"

9

The label came to me with a concept for the ". . . Baby One More Time" video in which I would play a futuristic astronaut. The mock-up I saw had me looking like a Power Ranger. That image didn't resonate with me, and I had a feeling my audience wouldn't relate to it, either. I told the executives at the label that I thought people would want to see my friends and me sitting at school, bored, and then as soon as the bell rang, *boom*—we'd start dancing.

The way the choreographer had us moving was so smooth. It helped that most of the dancers were from New York City. In the pop dance world, there are two camps. Most people will say that LA dancers are better. No disrespect to them, but my spirit has always liked New York dancers best—they have more heart. We rehearsed at Broadway Dance Center, where I'd taken classes as a kid, so I was comfortable there. When Jive

Records executive Barry Weiss came to the studio, I turned it on for him. In that moment, I showed him what I was capable of.

The director for the video, Nigel Dick, was open to my ideas. In addition to the school bell cuing the start of the dancing, I added that it was important that there be cute boys. And I thought we should wear school uniforms to make it seem more exciting when we started dancing outside in our casual clothes. We even got to cast Miss Fe as my teacher. I found it hilarious to see her in nerdy glasses and frumpy teacher clothes.

Making that video was the most fun part of doing that first album.

That's probably the moment in my life when I had the most passion for music. I was unknown, and I had nothing to lose if I messed up. There is so much freedom in being anonymous. I could look out at a crowd who'd never seen me before and think, *You don't know who I am yet*. It was kind of liberating that I didn't really have to care if I made mistakes.

For me, performing wasn't about posing and smiling. Onstage, I was like a basketball player driving down the court. I had ball sense, street sense. I was fearless. I knew when to take my shots.

Starting in the summer, Jive sent me on a mall tour—to something like twenty-six malls! Doing that form of promotion is not much fun. No one knew who I was yet. I had to try to sell myself to people who weren't that interested.

My demeanor was innocent—and it wasn't an act. I didn't know what I was doing. I'd just say, "Yeah, hi! My song's really good! You've got to check it out!"

Before the video came out, not a lot of people knew what I looked like. But by the end of September, the song was on the radio. I was sixteen when, on October 23, 1998, the ". . . Baby One More Time" single hit stores. The next month the video premiered, and suddenly I was getting recognized everywhere I went. On January 12, 1999, the album came out and sold over ten million copies very quickly. I debuted at number one on the Billboard 200 chart in the US. I became the first woman to debut with a number one single and album at the same time. I was so happy. And I could feel my life start to open up. I didn't have to perform in malls anymore.

Things were moving fast. I toured with NSYNC, including my old *Mickey Mouse Club* friend Justin Timberlake, in tour buses. I was always with my dancers or Felicia or one of my two managers, Larry Rudolph and Johnny Wright. I acquired a security guard named Big Rob, who was unbelievably sweet to me.

I became a regular on MTV's *Total Request Live. Rolling Stone* sent David LaChapelle to Louisiana to shoot me for the April cover story "Inside the Heart, Mind & Bedroom of a Teen Dream." When the magazine came out, the photos were controversial because the cover shot of me in my underwear holding a Teletubby played up how young I was. My mother seemed concerned, but I knew that I wanted to work with David LaChapelle again.

Every day was new. I was meeting so many exciting people! Right when "Baby" came out, I met singer-songwriter Paula Cole at a party in New York. She was about fourteen years older than me. Oh my God, I looked up to her so much—at first, just based on her appearance. She was the smallest thing, with the curliest brown hair flowing down her back. I had no idea who the hell she was, only that she was beautiful, with this incredible look and energy.

Years later I figured out that she was also the singer of songs I loved. When I first heard her voice, I thought she looked completely different than she actually did. Putting her angelic face to her super-dirty words on "Feelin' Love," her tiny body with the strength of her voice on "I Don't Want to Wait," I realized how powerful it can be when women defy expectations.

10

Justin Timberlake and I had stayed in touch after the *Mickey Mouse Club* and enjoyed spending time together on the NSYNC tour. Having shared that experience at such a young age gave us a shorthand. We had so much in common. We met up when I was on tour and started hanging out during the day before shows and then after shows, too. Pretty soon I realized that I was head over heels in love with him—so in love with him it was pathetic.

When he and I were anywhere in the same vicinity—his mom even said this—we were like magnets. We'd just find each other immediately and stick together. You couldn't explain the way we were together. It was *weird*, to be honest, how in love we were. His band, NSYNC, was what people back then called "so pimp." They were white boys, but they loved hip-hop. To me that's what separated them from the Backstreet

Boys, who seemed very consciously to position themselves as a white group. NSYNC hung out with Black artists. Sometimes I thought they tried too hard to fit in. One day J and I were in New York, going to parts of town I'd never been to before. Walking our way was a guy with a huge, blinged-out medallion. He was flanked by two giant security guards.

J got all excited and said, so loud, "Oh yeah, fo shiz, fo shiz! Ginuwiiiiiine! What's up, homie?"

After Ginuwine walked away, Felicia did an impression of J: "Oh yeah, fo shiz, fo shiz! Ginuwiiiiiine!"

J wasn't even embarrassed. He just took it and looked at her like, *Okay, fuck you, Fe.*

That was the trip where he got his first necklace—a big *T* for Timberlake.

I had a hard time being as carefree as he seemed. I couldn't help but notice that the questions he got asked by talk show hosts were different from the ones they asked me. Everyone kept making strange comments about my breasts, wanting to know whether or not I'd had plastic surgery.

Press could be uncomfortable, but at awards shows, I felt real joy. The child in me got a thrill seeing Steven Tyler from Aerosmith for the first time at the MTV Video Music Awards. I saw him coming in late, wearing something fantastic that looked like a wizard's cape. I gasped. It felt surreal to see him in person. Lenny Kravitz came in late, too. And, again, I thought, *Legends! Legends everywhere I look!*

I started running into Madonna all over the world. I would do shows in Germany and Italy, and we would end up performing at the same European awards shows. We'd greet each other as friends.

At one awards show, I knocked on Mariah Carey's dressing room door. She opened it and out poured the most beautiful, otherworldly light. You know how we all have ring lights now? Well, more than twenty years ago, only Mariah Carey knew about ring lights. And no, I can't say just her first name. To me she is always going to be *Mariah Carey*.

I asked if we could take a photo together and tried to take one where we were standing, and she said, "No! Come stand here, darling. This is my light. This is my side. I want you to stand here so I can get my good side, girl." She kept saying that in her deep, beautiful voice: "My *good* side, girl. My good *side*, girl."

I did everything Mariah Carey told me to do and we took the photo. Of course she was completely right about everything—the photo looked incredible. I know I won an award that night, but I couldn't even tell you what it was. The perfect photo with Mariah Carey—that was the real prize.

Meanwhile, I was breaking records, becoming one of the best-selling female artists of all time. People kept calling me the Princess of Pop.

At the 2000 VMAs, I sang the Rolling Stones' "(I Can't Get No) Satisfaction" and then "Oops! . . . I Did It Again" while going from a suit and hat to a glittery bikini top and tight pants, my long hair down. Wade Robson choreographed it—he always knew how to make me look strong and feminine at the same time. During the dance breaks in the cage, I did poses that made me look girly in the middle of an aggressive performance.

Later, MTV sat me down in front of a monitor and made me watch strangers in Times Square give their opinions of my performance. Some of them said I did a good job, but an awful lot of them seemed to be focused on my having worn a skimpy outfit. They said that I was dressing "too sexy," and thereby setting a bad example for kids.

The cameras were trained on me, waiting to see how I would react to this criticism, if I would take it well or if I would cry. *Did I do something wrong?* I wondered. I'd just danced my heart out on the awards show. I never said I was a role model. All I wanted to do was sing and dance.

The MTV show host kept pushing. What did I think of the commenters telling me I was corrupting America's youth?

Finally, I said, "Some of them were very sweet . . . But I'm not the children's parents. I just gotta be me. I know there are going to be people out there—I know not everyone's gonna like me."

It shook me up. And it was my first real taste of a backlash that would last years. It felt like every time I turned on an entertainment show, yet another person was taking shots at me, saying I wasn't "authentic."

I was never quite sure what all these critics thought I was supposed to be doing—a Bob Dylan impression? I was a teenage girl from the South. I signed my name with a heart. I liked looking cute. Why did everyone treat me, even when I was a teenager, like I was *dangerous*?

Meanwhile, I started to notice more and more older men in the audience, and sometimes it would freak me out to see them leering at me like I was some kind of Lolita fantasy for them, especially when no one could seem to think of me as both sexy and capable, or talented and hot. If I was sexy, they seemed to think I must be stupid. If I was hot, I couldn't possibly be talented.

I wish back then I'd known the Dolly Parton joke: "I'm not offended by all the dumb blonde jokes because I know I'm not dumb. And I also know that I'm not blonde." My real hair color is black.

Trying to find ways to protect my heart from criticism and to keep the focus on what was important, I started reading religious books like the Conversations with God series by Neale Donald Walsch. I also started taking Prozac.

* * *

When *Oops! . . . I Did It Again* came out, I was a household name and in control of my career. Around the time of my first world tour for *Oops!*, I was able to build my mom a house and settle my father's debts. I wanted to give them a clean slate.

11

There was hardly any time to rehearse. I only had a week to get ready. I was performing at the 2001 Super Bowl halftime show alongside Aerosmith, Mary J. Blige, Nelly, and NSYNC. Justin and the rest of his band had special gloves that shot fountains of sparks! I sang "Walk This Way" wearing a sexy version of a football uniform, with shiny silver pants, a crop shirt, and an athletic sock on one of my arms. I was brought to Steven Tyler's trailer to meet him right before the show, and his energy was incredible: he was such an idol to me. When we finished, the stadium lit up with fireworks.

The halftime show was just one of the seemingly endless good things happening for me. I landed the "most powerful woman" spot on the *Forbes* list of most powerful celebrities—the following year I'd be number one overall. I learned that tabloids were making so much money off photos of me, I was almost single-handedly keeping some magazines in business. And I was starting to get amazing offers.

At the 2001 MTV Video Music Awards that September, the plan was for me to sing "I'm a Slave 4 U," and we decided I would use a snake as a prop. It's become an iconic moment in VMAs history, but it was even more terrifying than it appeared.

The first time I saw the snake was when they brought it to a little back room of the Metropolitan Opera House in Manhattan, where we would be doing the show. The girl who handed it over was even smaller than me—she looked so young, and she was very tiny, with blond hair. I couldn't believe they didn't have some big guy in charge—I remember thinking, *You're letting us two little munchkins handle this huge snake . . . ?*

But there we were, and there was no going back: she lifted up the snake and put it over my head and around me. To be honest, I was a little scared—that snake was a huge animal, yellow and white, crinkly, gross-looking. It was okay because the girl who gave it to me was right there, plus a snake handler and a bunch of other people.

Everything changed, though, when I actually had to do the song onstage with the snake. Onstage I'm in performance mode: I'm in a costume, and there's nobody else there but me. Once again the little munchkin came to me and handed me that huge snake, and all I knew was to look down, because I felt if I looked up and caught its eye, it would kill me.

In my head I was saying, *Just perform, just use your legs and perform*. But what nobody knows is that as I was singing, the snake brought its head right around to my face, right up to me, and started hissing at me. You didn't see that shot on the TV, but in real life? I was thinking, *Are you fucking serious right now? The fucking goddamn snake's tongue is flicking out at me. Right. Now.* Finally, I got to the part where I handed it back, thank God.

The next night at Madison Square Garden in New York City, just days before September 11, I performed a duet of "The Way You Make Me Feel" with Michael Jackson to celebrate the thirtieth anniversary of his solo career. In my heels, I prowled all over that stage. The audience went *crazy*. At one point it felt like the whole crowd of twenty thousand was singing along with us.

Pepsi hired me to do commercials for them. In "The Joy of Pepsi," I started out as a delivery driver and then wound up in a huge dance number. In "Now and Then," I got to wear cute outfits from various eras. For the eighties section, I got made up as Robert Palmer for a version of "Simply Irresistible." I was in hair and makeup for *four hours*, and they still didn't quite manage to make me convincing as a man. But in the fifties part, I loved dancing at the drive-in. I had Betty Boop hair. Working in all those different genres, I was amazed at how intelligently done those commercials were.

*　　*　　*

The first movie I did was *Crossroads*, written by Shonda Rhimes and directed by Tamra Davis. We had filmed it in March 2001, around the same time I was recording the album *Britney*. In the film, I was playing a "good girl" named Lucy Wagner. The experience wasn't easy for me. My problem wasn't with anyone involved in the production but with what acting did to my mind. I think I started Method acting—only I didn't know how to break out of my character. I really became this other person. Some people do Method acting, but they're usually *aware of the fact that they're doing it*. But I didn't have any separation at all.

This is embarrassing to say, but it's like a cloud or something came over me and I just became this girl named Lucy. When the camera came on, I was her, and then I couldn't tell the difference between when the camera was on and when it wasn't. I know that seems stupid, but it's the truth. I took it that seriously. I took it seriously to the point where Justin said, "Why are you walking like that? Who *are* you?"

All I can say is it's a good thing Lucy was a sweet girl writing poems about how she was "not a girl, not yet a woman," and not a serial killer.

I ended up walking differently, carrying myself differently, talking differently. I was someone else for months while I filmed *Crossroads*. Still to this day, I bet the girls I shot that movie with think, *She's a little . . . quirky*. If they thought that, they were right.

I was a baby, just like the character. I should've played myself on camera. But I was so eager to do a good job that I kept trying to *go deep* with this character. I had been me my whole life, and I wanted to try something different! I should have said to myself, *It's a teen road movie. It's not that deep. Honestly, just have a good time.*

After the movie wrapped, one of my girlfriends from a club in LA came to visit me. We went to CVS. I swear to God, I walked into the store, and as I talked to her while we shopped, I finally came back to myself. When I came outside again I was cured of the spell that movie had cast. It was so strange. My little spirit showed back up in my body. That trip to buy makeup with a friend was like waving some magic wand.

Then I was pissed.

I thought, *Oh my God, what have I been doing the past few months? Who was I?*

That was pretty much the beginning and end of my acting career, and I was relieved. *The Notebook* casting came down to me and Rachel McAdams, and even though it would have been fun to reconnect with Ryan Gosling after our time on the *Mickey Mouse Club*, I'm glad I didn't do it. If I had, instead of working on my album *In the Zone* I'd have been acting like a 1940s heiress day and night.

I'm sure a lot of the problem was that it was my first experience with acting. I imagine there are people in the acting field who have dealt with something like that, where they had trouble separating themselves from a character. But I feel like they keep perspective. I hope I never get close to that occupational hazard again. Living that way, being half yourself and half a fictional character, is messed up. After a while you don't know what's real anymore.

12

When I think back on that time, I was truly living the dream, living *my* dream. My tours took me all over the world. One of my happiest moments on tour was playing the music festival Rock in Rio 3, in January 2001.

In Brazil, I felt liberated, like a child in some ways—a woman and a child all in one. I was fearless at that point, filled with a rush and a drive.

At night my dancers—there were eight of them, two girls, the rest guys—and I went skinny-dipping in the ocean, singing and dancing and laughing with each other. We talked for hours under the moon. It was so beautiful. Exhausted, we headed into the steam rooms, where we talked some more.

I was able to be a little bit sinful then—skinny-dipping, staying up talking all night—nothing over the top. It was a taste of rebellion, and freedom, but I was just having fun and being a nineteen-year-old.

The Dream Within a Dream Tour, right after my album *Britney* came out in the fall of 2001, was my fourth tour and one of my favorites. Every night onstage, I battled a mirror version of myself, which felt like it was probably a metaphor for something. But that mirror act was just one song. There was also flying! And an Egyptian barge! And a jungle! Lasers! Snow!

Wade Robson directed and choreographed it, and I give great credit to the people who put it together. I thought it was well conceived. Wade had this concept of the show as reflecting a new, more mature phase in my life. The set and costumes were so clever. When someone knew just how to style me, I was always grateful.

They were shrewd about how they presented me as a star, and I know that I owe them. The way they captured me showed they respected me as an artist. The minds behind that tour were brilliant. It was by far my best tour.

It was what we all had hoped for. I had worked so hard to get to that point. I'd done mall tours before *Baby* was released, then the *Baby* tour was the first time I got to see a lot of people out there in the crowd. I remember feeling like, *Oh, wow, I'm somebody now.* Then *Oops!* was a little bit bigger, so by the time I did the Dream Within a Dream Tour, it was all magic.

*   *   *

By the spring of 2002, I had hosted *SNL* twice, playing a butter churn girl at a colonial reenactment museum opposite Jimmy Fallon and Rachel Dratch and then playing Barbie's little sister, Skipper, opposite Amy Poehler as Barbie. I was the youngest person to host and perform as the musical guest in the same episode.

Around that time, I was asked if I'd like to be in a movie musical. I wasn't sure I wanted to act again after *Crossroads*, but I was tempted by this one. It was *Chicago*.

Executives involved in the production came to a venue where I was performing and asked if I wanted to do it. I'd turned down three or four movies, because I was in my moment with the stage show. I didn't want to be distracted from music. I was happy doing what I was doing.

But I look back now and I think, when it came to *Chicago*, I should've done it. I had power back then; I wish I'd used it more thoughtfully, been more rebellious. *Chicago* would have been fun. It's all dance pieces—my favorite kind: prissy, girly follies, Pussycat Doll–like, serve-off-your-corset moves. I wish I'd taken that offer.

I would have gotten to play a villain who kills a man, and sings and dances while doing it, too.

I probably could have found ways, gotten training, to keep from *becoming* a *Chicago* character the way I had with Lucy in

Crossroads. I wish I'd tried something different. If only I'd been brave enough not to stay in my safe zone, done more things that weren't just within what I knew. But I was committed to not rocking the boat, and to not complaining even when something upset me.

In my personal life, I was so happy. Justin and I lived together in Orlando. We shared a gorgeous, airy two-story house with a tile roof and a swimming pool out back. Even though we were both working a lot, we'd make time to be home together as often as we could. I always came back every few months so Justin and I could be together for two weeks, sometimes even two months, at a time. That was our home base.

One week, when Jamie Lynn was young, my family flew out to see us. We all went to FAO Schwarz at Pointe Orlando. They closed down the whole store for us. My sister got a miniature convertible car that had actual doors that opened. It was in between a real car and a go-kart. Somehow we got it back to Kentwood, and she drove it around the neighborhood until she outgrew it.

That child in that car was unlike anything else—this adorable little girl, driving around in a miniature red Mercedes. It was the cutest thing you could've ever seen in your entire life. I swear to God, the vision was unbelievable.

That's how we all were with Jamie Lynn: *You see it, you like it, you want it, you got it.* As far as I could tell, her world was the Ariana Grande song "7 Rings" come to life. (When I was growing up, we didn't have any money. My prized possessions were my Madame Alexander dolls. There were dozens to choose from. Their eyelids went up and down, and they all had names. Some were fictional characters or historical figures—like Scarlett O'Hara or Queen Elizabeth. I had the girls from *Little Women.* When I got my fifteenth doll, you would've thought I'd hit the lottery!)

That was a good time in my life. I was so in love with Justin, just *smitten.* I don't know if when you're younger love's a different thing, but what Justin and I had was special. He wouldn't even have to say anything or do anything for me to feel close to him.

In the South, moms love to round up the kids and say, "Listen, we're going to go to church today, and we're all going to color-coordinate." That's what I did when Justin and I attended the 2001 American Music Awards, which I cohosted with LL Cool J. I still can't believe that Justin was going to wear denim and I said, "We should match! Let's do denim-on-denim!"

At first, honestly, I thought it was a joke. I didn't think my stylist was actually going to do it, and I never thought Justin was going to do it with me. But they both went all in.

The stylist brought Justin's all-denim outfit, including a denim hat to match his denim jacket and denim pants. When he put it on, I thought, *Whoa! I guess we're really doing this!*

Justin and I were always going to events together. We had so much fun doing the Teen Choice Awards, and we often color-coordinated our outfits. But with the matching denim, we blew it up. That night my corset had me sucked in so tight under my denim gown, I was about to fall over.

I get that it was tacky, but it was also pretty great in its way, and I am always happy to see it parodied as a Halloween costume. I've heard Justin get flak for the look. On one podcast where they were teasing him about it, he said, "You do a lot of things when you're young and in love." And that's exactly right. We were giddy, and those outfits reflected that.

There were a couple of times during our relationship when I knew Justin had cheated on me. Especially because I was so infatuated and so in love, I let it go, even though the tabloids seemed determined to rub my face in it. When NSYNC went to London in 2000, photographers caught him with one of the girls from All Saints in a car. But I never said anything. At the time we'd only been together for a year.

Another time, we were in Vegas, and one of my dancers who'd been hanging out with him told me he'd gestured toward a girl and said, "Yeah, man, I hit that last night." I don't want to say who he was talking about because she's actually very popular and she's married with kids now. I don't want her to feel bad.

My friend was shocked and believed Justin was only saying it because he was high and felt like bragging. There were
rumors about him with various dancers and groupies. I let it
all go, but clearly, he'd slept around. It was one of those things
where you know but you just don't say anything.

So I did, too. Not a lot—*one* time, with Wade Robson. We
were out one night and we went to a Spanish bar. We danced
and danced. I made out with him that night.

I was loyal to Justin for years, only had eyes for him with
that one exception, which I admitted to him. That night was
chalked up to something that will happen when you're as
young as we were, and Justin and I moved past it and stayed
together. I thought we were going to be together forever. I
hoped we would be.

At one point when we were dating, I became pregnant
with Justin's baby. It was a surprise, but for me it wasn't a tragedy. I loved Justin so much. I always expected us to have a family together one day. This would just be much earlier than I'd
anticipated. Besides, what was done was done.

But Justin definitely wasn't happy about the pregnancy. He
said we weren't ready to have a baby in our lives, that we were
way too young.

I could understand. I mean, I *kind of* understood. If he
didn't want to become a father, I didn't feel like I had much
of a choice. I wouldn't want to push him into something he
didn't want. Our relationship was too important to me. And so

I'm sure people will hate me for this, but I agreed not to have the baby.

Abortion was something I never could have imagined choosing for myself, but given the circumstances, that is what we did.

I don't know if that was the right decision. If it had been left up to me alone, I never would have done it. And yet Justin was so sure that he didn't want to be a father.

We also decided on something that in retrospect wound up being, in my view, wrong, and that was that I should not go to a doctor or to a hospital to have the abortion. It was important that no one find out about the pregnancy or the abortion, which meant doing everything at home.

We didn't even tell my family. The only person who knew besides Justin and me was Felicia, who was always on hand to help me. I was told, "It might hurt a little bit, but you'll be fine."

On the appointed day, with only Felicia and Justin there, I took the little pills. Soon I started having excruciating cramps. I went into the bathroom and stayed there for hours, lying on the floor, sobbing and screaming. *They should've numbed me with something*, I thought. I wanted some kind of anesthesia. I wanted to go to the doctor. I was so scared. I lay there wondering if I was going to die.

When I tell you it was painful—I can't begin to describe it. The pain was unbelievable. I went down to the ground on my knees, holding the toilet. For a long time, I couldn't move. To this day, it's one of the most agonizing things I have ever experienced in my life.

Still, they didn't take me to the hospital. Justin came into the bathroom and lay on the floor with me. At some point he thought maybe music would help, so he got his guitar and he lay there with me, strumming it.

I kept crying and sobbing until it was all over. It took hours, and I don't remember how it ended, but I do, twenty years later, remember the pain of it, and the fear.

After that, I was messed up for a while, especially because I still did love Justin so much. It was insane how much I loved him, and for me it was unfortunate.

I should have seen the breakup coming, but I didn't.

13

When Justin began making his first solo album, *Justified*, he started being very standoffish with me. I think that was because he'd decided to use me as ammunition for his record, and so it made it awkward for him to be around me staring at him with all that affection and devotion. Ultimately, he ended our relationship by text message while I was on the set for the video for the "Overprotected" remix by Darkchild. After seeing the message as I sat in my trailer between takes, I had to go back out and dance.

For as much as Justin hurt me, there was a huge foundation of love, and when he left me I was *devastated*. When I say devastated, I mean I could barely *speak* for months. Whenever anyone asked me about him, all I could do was cry. I don't know if I was clinically in shock, but it felt that way.

Everyone who knew me thought something was wrong

with me, really wrong. I went back home to Kentwood, and I couldn't talk to my family or friends. I barely left the house. I was that messed up. I lay in my bed and stared at the ceiling.

Justin flew out to Louisiana to visit me. He brought me a long letter he'd written and framed. I still have it under my bed. And at the end it said—it makes me want to cry to think about it—"I can't breathe without you." Those are the last words in it.

Reading that, I thought, *Damn. He's a good writer.* Because that was exactly how I felt. It almost felt like I was suffocating, like I couldn't breathe, after all that had happened. The thing is, though, even after I saw him and read the letter, I didn't come out of the trance. He did all that, he came there to see me, and I still couldn't talk—to him or to anybody.

14

Even though the last thing I wanted to do was perform, I still had tour dates left in my contract, so I went back out to finish them. All I wanted was to get off the road: To have days and nights all to myself. To walk out onto the Santa Monica Pier and breathe in the salt air, listen to the rattle of the roller coaster, stare out at the ocean. Instead, every day was a grind. *Load in. Load out. Sound check. Photo shoot. Asking, "What town are we even in?"*

I'd loved the Dream Within a Dream Tour when it started, but it had become a slog. I was tired in mind and body. I wanted to shut it all down. I had begun fantasizing about opening a little shop in Venice Beach with Felicia and quitting show business completely. With the gift of hindsight, I can see that I hadn't given myself enough time to heal from the breakup with Justin.

*   *   *

In late July 2002, at the very end of the tour, we headed south to do a show in Mexico City. But getting there was almost a disaster.

We were traveling in vans, and once we'd crossed the border, we came to a sudden halt. We'd been stopped by a bunch of guys holding the biggest guns I'd ever seen. I was terrified; it felt like we were being ambushed. It just didn't make sense to me, but all I knew was we were surrounded by these angry-looking men. Everyone in my van was so tense; I had security with me, but who knew what was going to happen. After what felt like forever, there seemed to be some kind of peace talks happening—it was like in a movie. It's still a mystery to me what actually happened, but in the end, we were allowed to carry on, and we got to play to fifty thousand people (though the second show, on the following day, had to be canceled halfway through because of a massive thunderstorm).

That thunderstorm-canceled show was the last date of the Dream Within a Dream Tour, but when I told people after finishing the tour that I wanted to rest, everyone seemed nervous. When you're successful at something, there's a lot of pressure to keep right on doing it, even if you're not enjoying it anymore. And, as I would quickly find out, you really can't go home again.

I did an interview with *People* magazine back in Louisiana, for reasons that seemed ridiculous to me: I wasn't promoting anything, but my team thought I should show that I was doing well and "just taking a little break."

The photographer shot me outside, and then inside with the dogs and my mom on the couch. They had me empty out my purse to reveal that I wasn't carrying drugs or cigarettes: all they found was Juicy Fruit gum, vanilla perfume, mints, and a little bottle of St. John's wort. "My daughter is doing beautifully," my mom told the reporter confidently. "She's never, ever been close to a breakdown."

Part of what made that period of time so difficult is that Justin's family had been the only real, loving family I had. For holidays, the only family I would go to was his. I knew his grandmother and his grandfather, and I loved them so much. I thought of them as home. My mom would come out and visit us every once in a while, but she's not who I went *home* to, ever.

My mom was trying to recover from her divorce from my dad, which she'd finally gone through with; depressed and self-medicating, she could barely get up off the couch. My dad was nowhere to be found. And my little sister—well, when I tell you she was a *total bitch*, I'm not exaggerating.

I had always been the worker bee. While I was doing my thing on the road with Felicia, I hadn't been paying attention to what was happening in Kentwood. But when I came home, I saw how things had changed. My mom would serve Jamie Lynn while she watched TV, bringing her little chocolate milkshakes. It was clear that girl ruled the roost.

Meanwhile, it was like I was a ghost child. I can remember walking into the room and feeling like no one even saw me.

Jamie Lynn only saw the TV. My mother, who at one time had been the person I was closest to in the world, was on another planet.

And the way adolescent Jamie Lynn spoke to my mother—my mouth would just drop. I'd listen to her spew these hateful words, and I'd turn to my mother and say, "Are you going to let this little *witch* talk to you like that?" I mean, she was *bad*.

I felt betrayed by how Jamie Lynn had changed. I'd bought a house for Jamie Lynn to grow up in. She was not exactly grateful for it. She'd later say, "Why'd she get us a *house*?"—like it was some sort of imposition. But that house had been a gift. I'd bought it because our family had needed a new house, and I'd wanted her to have a better life than I had.

Life in Louisiana had passed me by. I felt like I had no one to talk to. Going through that breakup, going home and seeing how much I didn't fit in anywhere anymore, I realized that I was technically growing up, becoming a woman. And yet, honestly, it was almost like I went backward at the same time and became younger in my mind. Have you seen *The Curious Case of Benjamin Button*? That's how I felt. Somehow that year, in becoming more vulnerable I started to feel like a child again.

15

To get my confidence back, in September 2002 I went to Milan to visit Donatella Versace. That trip invigorated me— it reminded me that there was still fun to be had in the world. We drank amazing wine and ate amazing food. Donatella was a dynamic host. I was hoping things would turn around a little bit from that point.

She had invited me to Italy to attend one of her runway shows. Donatella dressed me in a beautiful sparkly rainbow dress. I was supposed to sing but I really didn't feel like it, so after I did a little bit of posing, Donatella said we could take it easy. She played my cover of Joan Jett's "I Love Rock 'n' Roll," I said hi to the models, and we were done.

Then it was time to party. Donatella is known for her lavish parties, and this one was no exception. I remember seeing Lenny Kravitz there, all these cool people. That party was really the first thing I did to put myself out there a bit after the breakup with Justin—on my own, innocent.

During the party I noticed a guy and I remember thinking he was so cute. He looked like he was probably Brazilian: dark hair, handsome, smoking a blunt—your typical bad boy. He was nothing like the LA actor types I'd known—he was more like a real man, the kind of man you have a one-night stand with. He was just sex.

When I first noticed him, he was off talking to these two girls, but I could tell he wanted to talk to me.

Eventually we started talking, and I decided I'd like to have drinks with him at my hotel. We headed to my car, but during the drive, he did something that just turned me off—honestly, I can't even remember what it was. But it was one little thing that really irritated me, so I told the driver to pull over, and without saying a word, I kicked the guy out on the side of the road and left him there.

Now that I'm a mom, I'd never do anything like that—I'd be more like "I'll drop you off at this place at this time . . ." But back then, at twenty years of age, it was pure instinct. I'd made a bad mistake letting this stranger inside my car, and I kicked him out.

Soon after my return, Justin was preparing to release his solo album *Justified*. On *20/20* he played an unreleased song for

Barbara Walters called "Don't Go (Horrible Woman)" that seemed to be about me: "I thought our love was so strong. I guess I was dead wrong. But to look at it positively, hey girl, at least you gave me a song about another Horrible Woman."

Less than a month later, he released the video for his song "Cry Me a River," in which a woman who looks like me cheats on him and he wanders around sad in the rain. In the news media, I was described as a harlot who'd broken the heart of America's golden boy. The truth: I was comatose in Louisiana, and he was happily running around Hollywood.

May I just say that on his explosive album and in all the press that surrounded it, Justin neglected to mention the several times he'd cheated on me?

There's always been more leeway in Hollywood for men than for women. And I see how men are encouraged to talk trash about women in order to become famous and powerful. But I was shattered.

The thought of my betraying him gave the album more angst, gave it a purpose: shit-talking an unfaithful woman. The hip-hop world of that era loved a storyline with the theme "Fuck you, bitch!" Getting revenge on women for perceived disrespect was all the rage at the time. Eminem's violent revenge song "Kim" was huge. The only problem with the narrative was that, in our case, it wasn't like that.

"Cry Me a River" did very well. Everyone felt very sorry for him. And it shamed me.

I felt there was no way at the time to tell my side of the story. I couldn't explain, because I knew no one would take my side once Justin had convinced the world of his version.

I don't think Justin realized the power he had in shaming me. I don't think he understands to this day.

After "Cry Me a River" came out, anywhere I went, I could get booed. I would go to clubs and I would hear boos. Once I went to a Lakers game with my little sister and one of my brother's friends, and the whole place, the whole arena, booed me.

Justin told everyone that he and I had had a sexual relationship, which some people have pointed out depicted me as not only a cheating slut but also a liar and hypocrite. Given that I had so many teenage fans, my managers and press people had long tried to portray me as an eternal virgin—never mind that Justin and I had been living together, and I'd been having sex since I was fourteen.

Was I mad at being "outed" by him as sexually active? No. To be honest with you, I liked that Justin said that. Why did my managers work so hard to claim I was some kind of young-girl virgin even into my twenties? Whose business was it if I'd had sex or not?

I'd appreciated it when Oprah told me on her show that my sexuality was no one else's business, and that when it came to virginity, "you don't need a world announcement if you change your mind."

Yes, as a teenager I played into that portrayal, because everyone was making such a big deal out of it. But if you think about it, it was pretty stupid for people to describe my body in that way, for them to point to me and say, "Look! A virgin!" It's nobody's business at all. And it took the focus off me as a musician and performer. I worked so hard on my music and on my stage shows. But all some reporters could think of to ask me was whether or not my breasts were real (they were, actually) and whether or not my hymen was intact.

The way Justin admitted to everyone that we'd had a sexual relationship broke the ice and made it so that I never had to come out myself as a non-virgin. His talking about our having had sex never bothered me at all, and I've defended him to people who criticized him for doing it. "That's so rude!" people have said about his talking about me sexually. But I liked it. What I heard when he said that was "She's a *woman*. No, she's not a virgin. Shut up."

As a child, I'd always had a guilty conscience, a lot of shame, a sense that my family thought I was just plain bad. The sadness and the loneliness that would hit me felt like my fault somehow, like I deserved unhappiness and bad luck. I knew the truth of our relationship was nothing like how it was being portrayed, but I still imagined that if I was suffering, I must have deserved it. Along the line, surely I'd done bad things. I believe in karma, and so when bad things happen, I imagine that it's just the law of karma catching up with me.

I've always been almost disturbingly empathic. What people are feeling in Nebraska, I can subconsciously feel even though I'm thousands of miles away. Sometimes women's periods sync up; I feel like my emotions are always syncing up with those around me. I don't know what hippie word you want to use for it—cosmic consciousness, intuition, psychic connection. All I know is that, 100 percent, I can feel the energy of other people. I can't help but take it in.

At this point, you might be saying to yourself, "Oh my God, is she really going to talk about this New Age stuff?"

Only for one more minute.

Because the point is, I was so sensitive, and I was so young, and I was still reeling from the abortion and the breakup; I didn't handle things well. Justin framed our time together with me as the bad guy, and I believed it, so ever since then, I've felt like I'm under a sort of curse.

And yet, I also started to hope that if that were true, if I had so much bad karma, it might be up to me—as an adult, as a woman—to reverse my luck, to bring myself good fortune.

I couldn't stand it anymore, so I escaped to Arizona with a girlfriend. That girlfriend happened to have been dating Justin's best friend, and we'd all broken up around the same time, so we'd decided to take a road trip to get away from all of it. We found each other and decided that we would leave it all behind.

Given what she'd been through, my friend was heartbroken, too, so we talked a lot, beside ourselves with grief and loneliness, and I was grateful for her friendship.

The sky overhead was full of stars while we drove fast through the desert, in a convertible with the top down, the wind blowing in our hair—no music playing, just the sound of the night whipping past us.

As we looked out at the road stretched before us, an eerie feeling settled over me. I had been moving so fast for so long, it was like I couldn't even catch my breath. Now, in this moment, something filled me: a profound beauty, otherworldly and humbling. I looked over at my friend, wondering if I should say something. But what could I say? "Do you believe in aliens?" So I stayed quiet and sat there with the feeling for a long moment.

Then I heard her voice over the wind.

"Do you feel that?" she said. She looked at me. "What *is* that?"

Whatever it was, she felt it, too.

I reached for her hand and held it tight.

The poet Rumi says the wound is the place where the light enters you. I have always believed that. The thing we felt that night in Arizona—we felt it at that moment because we needed it. We were so spiritually open and so raw. It showed us there was more than just what we could see—call it God, call it a higher power, or call it a paranormal experience. Whatever it was, it was real enough that we could experience it together. While it was first happening, I didn't want to bring it up to my friend because I was embarrassed. I was scared she would think that I'd lost my mind.

There have been so many times when I was scared to speak up because I was afraid somebody would think I was crazy. But I've learned that lesson now, the hard way. You have to speak the thing that you're feeling, even if it scares you. You have to tell your story. You have to raise your voice.

There was a lot I still had left to discover that night, when I was lost and felt God in the desert. But I knew that I wouldn't let the darkness consume me. Even in the darkest night, you can still find so much light.

16

Justin ended up sleeping with six or seven girls in the weeks after we officially broke up—or so I heard. Hey, I get it, he was Justin Timberlake. This was his first time to go solo. He was a girl's dream. I was in love with him. I understood the infatuation people had with him.

I decided if Justin was going to date, I should try to get out there, too. I hadn't dated in a while, since I'd been heartbroken and on tour. That winter I saw a guy who I thought was handsome, and a club promoter friend said I had good taste.

"That guy is so cool!" my friend said. "His name is Colin Farrell, and he's shooting a movie right now."

Well, talk about balls—I got in my car and I drove up to the set of his action movie, *S.W.A.T.* Who did I think I was?

There was no security or anything, so I went straight onto

the soundstage, where they were doing a set piece in a house. When the director saw me, he said, "Come sit in my chair!"

"Okay," I said. So I sat in the chair and watched them shoot. Colin came over and said, "Do you have any pointers for what I should do here?" He was inviting me to direct him.

We wound up having a two-week brawl. *Brawl* is the only word for it—we were all over each other, grappling so passionately it was like we were in a street fight.

In the course of our fun time together, he took me to the premiere of a spy thriller he was in called *The Recruit*, with Al Pacino. I was so flattered he asked me to go. I wore a pajama top. I thought it was a real shirt because it had miniature studs on it, but I see the photos and I think: *Yeah, I definitely wore a full-blown pajama top to Colin Farrell's premiere.*

I was so excited to be at the premiere. Colin's whole family was there, and they were so warm to me.

As I had before when I'd felt too attached to a man, I tried to convince myself in every way that it was not a big deal, that we were just having fun, that in this case I was vulnerable because I wasn't over Justin yet. But for a brief moment in time I did think there could be something there.

The disappointments in my romantic life were just one part of how isolated I became. I felt so awkward all the time.

I did try to be social. Natalie Portman—who I'd known since we were little girls in the New York theater circuit—and I even hosted a New Year's Eve party together.

But it took a huge amount of effort. Most days, I couldn't even bring myself to call a friend on the phone. The thought of going out and being brave onstage or at clubs, even at parties or dinners, filled me with fear. Joy around groups of other people was rare. Most of the time, I had serious social anxiety.

The way social anxiety works is that what feels like a totally normal conversation to most people, to you feels *mortifying*. Being around people at all, especially at a party or some other situation with expectations of presenting well, for no apparent reason causes surges of embarrassment. I was afraid of being judged or of saying something stupid. When that feeling hits, I want to be alone. I get scared and just want to excuse myself to the bathroom and then sneak out.

I veered between being very social and being incredibly isolated. I kept hearing that I seemed so confident. It was hard for anyone to imagine that someone who could perform for thousands at a time could, backstage with just one or two people, be gripped by panic.

Anxiety is strange that way. And mine grew as it became clear to me that whatever I did—and even plenty I didn't do—became front-page news. These stories were often illustrated by unflattering photos of me taken when I least expected it. I was already designed to care what others thought about me; the national spotlight turned my natural tendency to worry into something unbearable.

While the news about me was often not all that friendly,

the entertainment press was full of positive stories about Justin and Christina Aguilera. Justin was on the cover of *Rolling Stone* half-naked. Christina was on the cover of *Blender*, dressed like a madam from the Old West. They were together on the cover of *Rolling Stone*, him in a black tank top, looking at her with sexy eyes, her looking out at the camera, wearing a lace-up black shirt. In that story, she said she thought Justin and I should get back together, which was just confusing, given how negative she'd been elsewhere.

Seeing people I'd known so intimately talk about me that way in the press stung. Even if they weren't trying to be cruel, it felt like they were just pouring salt in the wound. Why was it so easy for everyone to forget that I was a human being— vulnerable enough that these headlines could leave a bruise?

Wanting to disappear, I found myself living in New York City alone for months, in a four-story NoHo apartment that Cher used to live in. It had tall ceilings, a terrace with a view of the Empire State Building, and a working fireplace much fancier than the one that had been in the living room of our house in Kentwood. It would have been a dream apartment to use as a home base to explore the city, but I hardly ever left the place. One of the only times I did, a man behind me on an elevator said something that made me laugh; I turned around and it was Robin Williams.

At one point, I realized I had somehow lost the key to the apartment. I was arguably the biggest star on earth, and I didn't even have a key to my own apartment. What a fucking idiot. I was stuck, both emotionally and physically; without a key, I couldn't go anywhere. I also wasn't willing to communicate with anyone. I had nothing to say. (But trust that I always have the key to my house these days.)

I didn't go to the gym. I didn't go out to eat. I only talked with my security guard and Felicia, who—now that I no longer needed a chaperone—had become my assistant and was still my friend. I fell off the face of the earth. I ate takeout for every meal. And this will probably sound strange, but I was content staying home. I liked it there. I felt safe.

On rare occasions, I went out. One night I put on a $129 Bebe dress and high heels, and my cousin took me to a sexy underground club with low ceilings and red walls. I took a couple hits from a joint, my first time smoking pot. Later, I walked all the way home so I could take in the city, breaking one of my heels along the way. When I got to my apartment, I went to my terrace and just looked up at the stars for hours. At that moment, I felt one with New York.

One of my few visitors during that strange, surreal time was Madonna. She walked into the place and immediately, of course, she owned the room. I remember thinking, *It's Madonna's room now*. Stunningly beautiful, she exuded power and confidence. She walked straight to the window, looked out, and said, "Nice view."

"Yeah, it's a nice view, I guess," I said.

Madonna's supreme confidence helped me see a lot about my situation with fresh eyes. I think she probably had some intuitive sense of what I was going through. I needed a little guidance at that time. I was confused about my life. She tried to mentor me.

At one point, she did a red-string ceremony with me to initiate me into Kabbalah, and she gave me a trunk full of *Zohar* books to pray with. At the base of my neck, I tattooed a word in Hebrew that means one of the seventy-two names of God. Some Kabbalists think of it as meaning *healing*, which was the thing I was still trying to do.

In many ways, Madonna did have a good effect on me. She told me I should be sure to take time out for my soul, and I tried to do that. She modeled a type of strength that I needed to see. There were so many different ways to be a woman in the industry: you could get a reputation for being a diva, you could be professional, or you could be "nice." I had always tried so hard to please—to please my parents, to please audiences, to please everyone.

I must have learned that helplessness from my mom. I saw the way my sister and my dad treated her and how she just took it. Early in my career, I followed that model and became passive. I wish I'd had more of a mentor then to be a badass bitch for me so I could've learned how to do that sooner. If I could go back now, I would try to become my own parent, my own partner, my own advocate—the way I knew Madonna did. She had endured so much sexism and bullying from the public and the industry, and had been shamed for her sexuality so many times, but she always overcame it.

When Madonna accepted her Billboard Woman of the Year award a few years ago, she said she'd been subjected to "blatant misogyny, sexism, constant bullying, and relentless abuse . . . If you're a girl, you have to play the game. What is that game? You're allowed to be pretty, and cute, and sexy. But don't act too smart. Don't have an opinion."

She's right that the music industry—really the whole world— is set up more for men. Especially if you're "nice," like me, you can be completely destroyed. By that point, I'd become almost too nice. Everywhere I went, Felicia would write thank-you notes to the chef, the bartender, the secretary. To this day, as a Southern girl, I believe in a handwritten thank-you note.

Madonna saw how much I wanted to please and how I wanted to do what others did instead of locking something down and saying, "Okay, everyone! Listen up! This is what's going to happen."

We decided to perform together at the VMAs.

Every time we rehearsed it, we did an air kiss. About two minutes before the performance, I was sitting on the side of the stage and thinking about my biggest performance to date at the VMAs, when I'd pulled off a suit to reveal a sparkly outfit. I thought to myself: *I want a moment like that again this year. With the kiss, should I just go for it?*

A lot was made of that kiss. Oprah asked Madonna about it. The kiss was treated as a huge cultural moment—"Britney kissing Madonna!"—and it got us both a lot of attention.

While we were rehearsing for the VMAs, I'd also had an idea for a collaboration. In the Culver City studio, my team and I were sitting on silver metal folding chairs, talking about how the record company was lukewarm on my new song "Me Against the Music"—a song I loved. I'd just done "I'm a Slave 4 U" on my last record, and Barry Weiss, who ran my label, wanted more songs like that. But I was pushing for "Me Against the Music"—hard.

"Then what if we do a feature on it?" I said. A song can become a massive hit because of the event that drives it. I thought if we could find someone to be on the song, we could create a story around it.

"Who do you want to feature?" my manager asked.

"Her!" I said, pointing across the room at Madonna. "Let's get her on the song."

"Holy shit," he said. "Yeah—that'd work." Instead of asking through her team, we agreed that I would ask her directly.

So I went over to Madonna. "Let's talk," I said. I told her how much fun it would be to do the song with me and how

I thought we could help each other: it was something that would benefit us both. She agreed.

"Me Against the Music" is still one of my favorite songs, and the collaboration with her is part of what makes it so memorable.

On the first day of our shoot for the song's video, which was to last two or three days, we were told a seam had come undone on Madonna's white suit and a seamstress had to be called to fix it, so there would be a delay in our start time. I wound up having to sit in my trailer for hours waiting for the suit to be fixed.

Really? I thought. I didn't even know taking so much time for oneself was an option. If I broke a heel on my shoe, I would never make production take the five minutes to let me fix it. I would do whatever the director told me to do, even if I had to hobble onto the set without a heel, even if I had to show up barefoot.

During our shoot together, I was in awe of the ways Madonna would not compromise her vision. She kept the focus on her. Going along with Madonna's ideas and being on her time for days was what it meant to collaborate with her. It was an important lesson for me, one that would take a long time for me to absorb: she demanded power, and so she got power. She was the center of attention because she made that the condition of her showing up anywhere. She made that life for herself. I hoped I could find ways to do that while preserving the parts of my nice-girl identity that I wanted to keep.

17

I was happy with my new album, *In the Zone*. "Me Against the Music," featuring Madonna, was the first single off the album. The next single was "Toxic," for which I won a Grammy Award. "Toxic" was innovative as well as a massive success, and is still one of my favorites to perform.

To promote the album, I went out with an MTV camera crew in New York City one night to film a special called *In the Zone & Out All Night*. We drove all over the city to appear at three nightclubs—Show, Splash, and Avalon. It was electrifying to see large groups of people dancing to the new songs. As has happened again and again in my career, my fans reminded me why I do what I do.

But then, one day, there was a knock on my door. When I opened it, four men just walked in right past me; I didn't recognize three of them. I'd never seen their faces before in my life.

The fourth was my father.

They proceeded to sit me down on a sofa (the same one I have to this day in my bedroom). Immediately they started peppering me with questions, questions, and more questions. I was mute: I wasn't willing to talk with anyone. I had nothing to say.

A day later I got a call from my team that I was going to speak to Diane Sawyer . . . and on that same sofa. Because of what had happened with Justin, and everything I'd been through, I felt like I was no longer able to communicate with the world. I had a dark cloud over my head; I was traumatized.

I'd often retreated to my apartment to be alone; now I was being forced to speak to Diane Sawyer there and cry in front of the entire nation.

It was completely humiliating. I wasn't told what the questions would be ahead of time, and it turned out they were 100 percent embarrassing. I was too vulnerable then, too sensitive, to do this type of interview. She asked things like, "He's going on television and saying you broke his heart. You did something that caused him so much pain. So much suffering. What did you do?"

I didn't want to share anything private with the world. I didn't owe the media details of my breakup. I shouldn't have been forced to speak on national TV, forced to cry in front of this stranger, a woman who was relentlessly going after me with harsh question after harsh question. Instead, I felt like I had been exploited, set up in front of the whole world.

That interview was a breaking point for me internally—a switch had been flipped. I felt something dark come over my body. I felt myself turning, almost like a werewolf, into a Bad Person.

I honestly feel like that moment in my life should have been a time for growing—and not sharing everything with the world. It would have been the better way to heal.

But I had no choice. It seemed like nobody really cared how I felt.

Back home in Louisiana again for the holidays, I invited some friends over. We were trying to hang out in the guesthouse I'd built behind the main house—and my mother got annoyed with us for being noisy. Suddenly, it hit me that I had enough money that we did not have to stay in Louisiana. I booked us a trip to Las Vegas for New Year's Eve and some friends from my tour joined us.

We cut loose at the Palms Casino Resort and drank—a *lot*. I'll admit that we got phenomenally stupid. I will also say that this was one time when I almost felt overwhelmed having that much freedom in Sin City. I was this little girl who had worked so much, and then all of a sudden the schedule was blank for a few days, and so: *Hello, alcohol!*

Paris Hilton showed up at the casino to hang out and have some drinks. Before I knew it, we got on top of tables, took our shoes off, and ran through the whole club like fairy-dusted idiots. No one got hurt, and I had the best time with Paris—we were just playing, and we still do every time we get together.

I wasn't rude to anybody. It was just innocent fun. Most people will probably judge, and now you can't do things like that because people will all whip their cameras out. But back then, that time in Vegas, we just acted silly. Having already been under so much media scrutiny, I wasn't interested in causing trouble—it was about feeling free and enjoying what I had been working so hard to achieve.

As a twentysomething will do after a few drinks, I wound up in bed with one of my old friends—a childhood friend who I'd known forever. The third night we were there together, he and I got shitfaced. I don't even remember that night at all, but from what I've pieced together, he and I lounged around the hotel room and stayed up late watching movies—*Mona Lisa Smile* and *The Texas Chainsaw Massacre*—then had the brilliant idea of going to A Little White Chapel at three thirty in the morning. When we got there, another couple was getting married, so we had to wait. Yes—we waited in line to get married.

People have asked me if I loved him. To be clear: he and I were not in love. I was just honestly very drunk—and probably, in a more general sense at that time in my life, very bored.

The next day, my whole family flew out to Vegas. They showed up and stared at me with these eyes of such fury. I looked around. "What happened last night?" I asked. "Did I kill someone?"

"You got *married*!" they said, as if that might be somehow worse.

"We were just having fun," I said.

But my mom and dad took it so seriously.

"We have to get this annulled," they said. They made way too big of a deal out of innocent fun. Everybody has a different perspective on it, but I didn't take it that seriously. I thought a goof-around Vegas wedding was something people might do as a joke. Then my family came and acted like I'd started World War III. I cried the whole rest of the time I was in Las Vegas.

"I'm guilty!" I said. "I'm so sorry. I shouldn't have gotten married."

We signed all the documents they told us to sign. The marriage lasted fifty-five hours. I thought it was strange they got so involved so quickly and so decisively—without my even having time to quite regret what I'd done.

It wasn't that I wanted to start a family with this guy or to be with him forever; it was nothing like that. And yet what happened was that my parents interrogated me so much about it that part of me almost said, "Hey, maybe I do want to be married!"

Every young person knows what it feels like to want to rebel against your family, especially if they're controlling. I now feel like I was having a very human reaction. They were putting a curious amount of pressure on me about something I thought was innocuous—and in any case, that was my own business.

In fact, my family was so against the wedding that I started to think maybe I'd accidentally committed a brilliant act. Because I realized: something about my being under their control and not having a stronger connection to someone else had become very, very important to them.

What do I have over you guys? I wondered. *Why would someone else be so huge a threat?* Perhaps it's worth mentioning that, by this point, I was supporting them financially.

Everyone was asking me—where do you go from here? And it was a good question. I had the answer. I told interviewers again and again that what I most wanted was some time to myself. I'd started to dream about finding true love and settling down. I felt like I'd been missing out on life.

18

We hit the road once again. More buses. More costume racks. More long rehearsals. More step-and-repeats.

That was already one of the darkest times of my life, and the vibe of the tour was dark, too—a lot of sweaty numbers, dark themes, and moody lighting. The tour also marked a change in my relationship with my brother, Bryan.

Working now as part of my team, Bryan was very well paid—and so was I—for the Onyx Hotel Tour. He also did a huge deal for me with Elizabeth Arden. And yet, I had trouble not resenting him a bit once I went out on what was to be an unbelievably grueling tour while he stayed in Los Angeles and New York and enjoyed his life.

I lost track of my brother in those years. And so, in many ways, it felt as though I lost Justin and Bryan around the same time.

The tour felt so depressing. In Moline, Illinois, I hurt my knee really badly toward the end of the show. I'd had a previous knee injury while rehearsing for the music video for "Sometimes" off my first album. That was more extreme: I'd cried hysterically. With this injury, I only had to reschedule two dates, but in my mind, I'd already started to check out. I was craving some lightness and joy in my life.

Then Kevin Federline was holding me. That's the thing I remember best. We met at a club called Joseph's Café in Hollywood, where I used to sit at a table in the back. Right away, from the moment I saw him, there was a connection between us—something that made me feel like I could escape everything that was hard in my life. That very first night we met, he held me—and I mean *held me*—in a pool for hours.

That was how he was to me: steady, strong, a comfort. I remember we would go swimming, and he'd just wrap his arms around me in the water and not let me go until I wanted him to, no matter how long that took. It was beyond a sexual thing. It wasn't about lust. It was *intimate*. He would hold me as long as I wanted to be held. Had anyone in my life ever done that before? If so, I couldn't remember when. And was there anything better?

After what I'd gone through with J, I hadn't been with someone in a real way in so long. Meanwhile, the press kept suggesting famous men who I should date—royalty, CEOs, models. How could I explain that I just wanted to be held for an hour by a man in a swimming pool?

I feel like a lot of women—and this is definitely true of me—can be as strong as they want to be, can play this powerful role, but at the end of the day, after we've done our work and made our money and taken care of everyone else, we want someone to hold us tight and tell us everything's going to be okay. I'm sorry. I know it sounds regressive. But I think it's a human impulse. We want to feel safe and alive and sexy all at the same time. And that's what Kevin did for me. So I held on to him like there was no tomorrow.

In the beginning, my relationship with Kevin was playful.

Kevin liked me the way I was. As a woman who'd spent so much time trying to live up to society's expectations, being with a man who gave me permission to be exactly who I was felt like such a gift.

Kevin had a "bad boy" image. Still, I had no idea when we met that he had a toddler, nor that his ex-girlfriend was eight months pregnant with his second baby. I was clueless. I was living in a bubble, and I didn't have a lot of good, close friends to confide in and get advice from. I had no idea until after we'd been together for a while and someone told me, "You know he has a new baby, right?"

I didn't believe it, but when I asked, he told me it was true. He told me he saw them once a month.

"You have *kids*?" I said. "You have *children*? Not only *one child* but *two children*?"

So, a number was done on me, obviously. I had no idea.

That spring of 2004 I had to go back to work to make good on my contracted dates, even though I was in no mood to do it. I figured it would be tolerable if Kevin could go with me, and he agreed to come. We had so much fun together on that tour; he helped keep me distracted from the work, which felt as challenging as it ever had. After the shows, I didn't have to go back to my hotel room alone. Flying home, we were chatting away, and I asked him to marry me. He said no and then *he* proposed.

We filmed tour diaries together. The original concept was a documentary like Madonna's *Truth or Dare*, but it became more like a collection of our home movies, especially after I got hurt again, and it was later released as a reality show called *Britney and Kevin: Chaotic*.

The Onyx Hotel Tour was just rough. It was too sexual, for a start. Justin had embarrassed me publicly, so my rebuttal onstage was to kind of go there a little bit, too. But it was absolutely horrible. I hated it in the moment. In fact, I hated that entire stupid tour—so much that I prayed every night. I said,

"God, just make my arm break. Make my leg break. Can you make *something* break?" And then, on June 8, 2004, with still two months of shows to go, I fell again on the set of my video for "Outrageous," got another knee injury, and had to have surgery. The rest of the tour dates were scrapped. I thought back on how much I'd suffered as a teenager doing physical therapy for my knee. The experience had been excruciating. I had to move my legs up and down even as they were causing me unspeakable agony. So when the doctors offered me Vicodin, I took it. I didn't want to experience that level of pain again.

I just went to my apartment in Manhattan, got into my princess bed, and if anyone—friends, family, people in the business—wanted to talk to me during this time, I said, "Leave me alone. No, I don't want to do anything or see anyone." And I definitely didn't want to go back out on tour for a while if I could help it.

Part of it was that I believed I had earned the right to make my own decisions in my personal life after such a grueling schedule. I felt like I'd been manipulated into going straight back to work after the breakup with Justin, because it was all I knew. The Onyx tour was a mistake. But in my mind I thought I should just do what I was supposed to do, which was work.

I realize now that I should've sat back and taken my time getting over the breakup with Justin before I resumed touring. The music industry is just too hard-core and unforgiving. You often visit a different city every day. There's no consistency. It's not possible to find stillness when you're on the road. When I made the *Britney Spears: Live and More!* video special in Hawaii in 2000, I began to realize that TV is really easy. TV is the luxury part of the business; touring is not.

My sister had also just landed a huge Nickelodeon deal. I was happy for her. Seeing her learning her lines and doing wardrobe fittings reminded me that I would have loved to have a job that was more like the cozy world of children's television. I liked thinking about the *Mickey Mouse Club* and remembering how easy everything had seemed back then.

I thought Kevin would give me the stability I was craving—and the freedom, too.

Not a lot of people were happy for Kevin and me. Whether or not I liked it, I was one of the biggest stars in the world at that time. He was living a more private life. I had to defend our relationship to everyone.

Kevin and I got married that fall. We held a "surprise" ceremony in September, but the lawyers needed more time with the prenup, so the legal event didn't take place for a couple weeks.

People shot the ceremony. I wore a strapless dress and the bridesmaids wore burgundy. After the ceremony, I changed into a pink sweatsuit that read MRS. FEDERLINE and everyone else put on Juicy tracksuits, too, because we went to a club after to dance all night. Now that I was married and thinking about starting a family, I decided to start saying no to things that didn't feel right—like the Onyx tour. I parted ways with my managers. I posted a letter to fans on my website in which I told them I was going to take some time off to enjoy my life.

"I've actually learned to say 'NO!' " I wrote, and I meant it. "With this newly found freedom, it's like people don't know how to act around me . . . I'm sorry that my life seemed like it was all over the place the past two years. It's probably because IT WAS! I understand now what they mean when they talk about child stars. Going and going and going is all I've ever known since I was fifteen years old . . . Please remember that times are changing and so am I."

I felt so much peace after announcing my intention to control my own life at last.

Things are going to change around here! I thought excitedly.

And then they did.

19

Two things about being pregnant: I loved sex and I loved food. Both of those things were absolutely amazing throughout both of my pregnancies.

Other than that, I can't say there was much that brought me any pleasure. I was just *so mean*. You did not want to hear from me those whole two years. I did not want to be around almost anyone at all. I was hateful. I didn't want anyone, not even my mom, to come near me. I was a real mama bear. America's sweetheart and the meanest woman alive.

I was protective over Jamie Lynn, too. After she complained to me about a costar of hers on her TV show, I showed up on the set to have words with the actress. What I must have looked like, hugely pregnant, yelling at a teenage (and, I would later learn, innocent) girl, "Are you spreading rumors about my sister?" (To that young actress: I'm sorry.)

When I was pregnant, I wanted everyone to stay away: *Stand back! There's a baby here!*

It's true what they say—when you have a baby, no one can prepare you. It's a miracle. You're creating another *body*. You grow up saying: "That person's pregnant." "That person had a baby." But when you actually experience it yourself, it's overwhelming. It was such a spiritual experience—such an incredibly powerful bond.

My mother had always talked about how painful childbirth was. She never let me forget that she'd been in many hours of agonizing labor with me. I mean, everybody's different. Some women have an easy time of it. I was terrified of giving birth naturally. When the doctor offered me a C-section, I was so relieved.

Sean Preston was born on September 14, 2005. Right away you could tell he was just a sweet, kind little boy.

Then, three months later, I got pregnant again. I was thrilled that I'd have two kids so close in age. Still, it was hard on my body, and there was a lot of sadness and loneliness in that time. I felt like so much of the world was against me.

The main danger I had to watch out for was the aggression of the paparazzi.

If I stayed out of the public eye, surely, eventually, I thought, the photographers would leave me alone. But whether I was sitting at home or trying to go to a store, photographers found me. Every day, and all night, they were there, waiting for me to come out.

What no one in the media seemed to realize was that I was hard on myself as it was. I could be wild, but at heart, I was always a people-pleaser. Even at my lowest, I cared what people thought. I grew up in the South, where manners are so important. I still, to this day, regardless of their age, call men "sir" and women "ma'am." Just on the level of civility, it was incredibly painful to be treated with such disregard—such disgust.

Everything I did with the babies was chronicled. When I drove off to escape the paparazzi with Sean Preston on my lap, that was taken as proof that I was unfit. I got cornered by the paparazzi with him at the Malibu Country Mart, too—they kept on taking my picture as, trapped, I held him and cried.

As I was trying to get out of a building and into a car in New York, pregnant with Jayden James and carrying Sean Preston, I was swarmed by photographers. I was told I had to get into the car on the other side, so I said, "Oh," and made my way through another thousand camera shutters and shouts of "Britney! Britney!" to get in there.

If you watch the video and don't just look at the still photos, you can see that while carrying a cup of water in one hand and my baby in the other arm, my heel turned and I almost went down—but I didn't fall. And in catching myself, I didn't drop either the water or the baby—who, by the way, was completely unfazed.

"This is why I need a gun," I said to the camera, which probably didn't go over that well. But I was at my wits' end. The magazines seemed to love nothing more than a photo they could run with the headline "Britney Spears got HUGE! Look, she's not wearing makeup!" As if those two things were some kind of a sin—as if gaining weight was something unkind I'd done to them personally, a betrayal. At what point did I promise to stay seventeen for the rest of my life?

20

When Sean Preston was very little, Kevin started working harder on his own music. He wanted to make his own name, which was something I encouraged. He was recording a lot, which was his passion. Sometimes I'd drop by a studio where he was working and it seemed like a clubhouse. I could smell the weed wafting out of the studio door before I even walked in. He and the other guys would all be getting high, and it felt like I was in the way. I wasn't invited to their party.

I couldn't stand being around pot smoke. Even the smell of it nauseated me. And I had the baby and was pregnant, so it wasn't like I could hang out all day. So mostly, I stayed home. It's not as if that was such a hardship. I had a beautiful home—a dream home. We would hire an amazing chef—too expensive to use very often. But one time, eating something the chef cooked, I said, "Oh my God, this is the most delicious thing

I've ever had and can you just live with us? I love you so much!"
And I meant it—I *loved* him. I was so grateful for any additional
help around the house.

Maybe this is the way married couples are, I thought as Kevin
and I grew more and more estranged. *You take turns letting each
other be a little selfish. This is his first taste of fame for himself. I should
let him have it.*

I gave myself pep talks: *He's my husband. I'm supposed to respect him, accept him on a deeper level than I'd accept someone I was
just dating. He's the father of my kids. His demeanor is different now,
but if it changed, it could change back. People say he's going to break
up with me while I have tiny children, like he did with the mother of
his first two children when they were infants, but no way! How he was
with his other family won't be the way he is with me.*

In trying to make up all these excuses in my head, I was
lying to myself—totally in denial this whole time that he was
leaving me. I flew to New York to see him. He'd been so out
of touch that I thought we needed to have some time together
as a family. In the city, I checked into a nice hotel, excited to
see my husband.

But he wouldn't see me. It seemed like he wanted to pretend I didn't exist.

His manager, who had been on my team for years, wouldn't
see me, either. He was on Kevin's team now and it seemed they
were done with me.

"Damn, really?" I said.

All I could think was that I wanted to get close enough to Kevin that I could ask him what was going on. I wanted to say, "When you left to come out here, we hugged. You kissed me. What's going on? What happened?"

I'd suspected something was up, that he was changing, especially once he started getting press and feeling himself. One time he came home late and told me he'd been at a party. "Justin Timberlake was there!" he said. "Lindsay Lohan was, too!"

Do you think I care about your stupid party? I thought. *Do you have any idea how many parties like that I've gone to? I've known some of those people longer than I've known you. Do you know how much I went through in my years with Justin? No—you know none of it.* I didn't say any of that, but I wanted to say it and a whole lot more.

Kevin was just so enthralled with the fame and the power. Again and again in my life I've seen fame and money ruin people, and I saw it happen with Kevin in slow motion. In my experience, when most people—especially men—get that type of attention, it's all over. They love it too much. And it's not good for them.

Some celebrities handle fame well. They have perspective. They have fun being admired but not too much fun. They know whose opinion to listen to and whose opinion to ignore. Getting awards and trophies is cool, and in the beginning—those first two years when you become a celebrity—well, it's a feeling you can't explain. I think some people are great at fame.

I'm not. My first two or three years I was good at it, and it was fine, but my real self? In school I was a basketball player. I didn't cheerlead, I didn't wanna be out there. I played ball. That's what I loved.

But fame? That world isn't real, my friends. It's. Not. Real. You go along with it because of course it's going to pay the family's bills and everything. But for me, there was an essence of real life missing from it. I think that's why I had my babies.

So getting awards and all that fame stuff? I liked it a lot. But there's nothing lasting in it for me. What I love is sweat on the floor during rehearsals, or just playing ball and making a shot. I like the work. I like the practicing. That has more authenticity and value than anything else.

I actually envy the people who know how to make fame work for them, because I hide from it. I get very shy. For example, Jennifer Lopez, from the beginning, struck me as someone who was very good at being famous—at indulging people's interest in her but knowing where to draw lines. She always handled herself well. She always carried herself with dignity.

Kevin didn't know how to do any of that. I'll confess, I'm not great at it, either. I'm a nervous person. I run away from most kinds of attention as I've gotten older, maybe because I've been really hurt.

At the time of that rough trip to New York, I should have known my marriage was over, but I still thought it might be salvageable. Later, Kevin moved on to another studio, this one in Las Vegas. And so I went there, hoping to talk to him.

When I found him, he had his head shaved. He was getting ready to shoot the cover for his album. He was in the studio all the time. He really thought he was a rapper now. Bless his heart—because he did take it so seriously.

And so I showed up in Vegas carrying Sean Preston, still pregnant with Jayden James, full of sympathy for Kevin's situation. He was trying to make something happen for himself and everyone seemed to be doubting him. I knew what that was like. It is scary to put yourself out there like that. You do really have to believe in yourself even when the world makes you wonder if you have what it takes. But I also felt like he should have been checking in more and should have been spending time with me. Our little family was my heart. I'd had his babies inside of me for a very long time, and I'd sacrificed a lot. I had all but abandoned my career. I had done everything to make our life possible.

I left Sean Preston at the hotel with a nanny and I showed up at the video set. Again, I was told that he didn't want to see me. He's since said that this isn't true, that he never would have done that. All I know is what I experienced: security guards who'd worked at my home were at the door and wouldn't let me in. It felt like everyone on that set was shunning me.

I peeked through a window and saw a bunch of young

people partying. The set had been turned into a nightclub. Kevin and the other actors were smoking weed and looking happy.

I felt completely outside of myself. I watched the scene for a while without anyone inside seeing me. Then I said to the security guard, "Okay, great," turned around, and went back to the hotel.

I was at the hotel, devastated, when there was a knock on the door.

I answered and it was one of my brother's old friends—Jason Trawick. He'd heard what had happened.

"How are you doing?" he asked. He seemed to genuinely care how I answered.

When was the last time someone asked me that? I wondered.

21

Right around Sean Preston's first birthday, on September 12, 2006, Jayden James came along. He was such a happy kid right from birth.

Once I'd had both the boys, I felt so *light*—so light it was almost like I was a bird or a feather, like I could float away.

My body felt incredible to me. *Is this what it's like to be a thirteen-year-old again?* I thought. I didn't have a belly anymore.

One of my friends came over and said, "Wow, you look so skinny!"

"Well, I've been pregnant for two years straight," I said.

After the babies, I felt like a completely different person. It was confusing.

On one hand, I suddenly fit into my clothes again. When I tried things on they looked good! Loving clothes again was a revelation. I thought, *Holy shit! My body!*

On the other hand, I'd been so happy feeling these babies protected inside me. I got a little depressed once I was no longer keeping them safe inside my body. They seemed so vulnerable out in the world of jockeying paparazzi and tabloids. I wanted them back inside me so the world couldn't get at them.

"Why is Britney so camera-shy with Jayden?" one headline read.

Kevin and I had gotten better at hiding the kids after Jayden was born, so much so that people were wondering why no pictures of him had been released. I think if anyone had thought about that question for a second, they could have come up with some guesses. But no one was really asking the question. They just kept acting like I owed it to them to let the men who kept trying to catch me looking fat take photos of my infant sons.

After each birth, one of the first things I had to do was look out the window to count the number of enemy combatants in the parking lot. They just seemed to multiply every time I checked. There were always more cars than seemed safe. To see that many men gathering to shoot photos of my babies—it made my blood run cold. With a whole lot of money in photo royalties on the line, it was their mission to get pictures of the boys at any cost.

And my boys—they were so tiny. It was my job to keep them safe. I worried that the flashing lights and the shouting would scare them. Kevin and I had to devise strategies to cover them with blankets while making sure they could still breathe. Even without a blanket over me, I barely could.

I didn't have much interest in doing press that year, but I did one interview, with Matt Lauer for *Dateline*. He said that people were asking questions about me, including: "Is Britney a bad mom?" He never said who was asking them. Everyone, apparently. And he asked me what I thought it would take for the paparazzi to leave me alone. I wished he'd ask them—so whatever it was, I could do exactly that.

Luckily, my home was a safe haven. Our relationship was in trouble, but Kevin and I had built an incredible house in Los Angeles, right beside Mel Gibson's house. Sandy from *Grease* lived nearby, too. I'd see her and call out, "Hi, Olivia Newton-John! How are you, Olivia Newton-John?"

For us, it was a dream house. There was a slide that went into the pool. There was a sandbox, full of toys, so the kids could build sandcastles. We had a miniature playhouse with steps and a ladder and a miniature porch. And we just kept adding on to it.

I didn't like the wooden floors so I added marble everywhere—and, of course, it had to be white marble.

The interior designer was completely against it. He said, "Marble floors are super slippery and hard if you fall down."

"I want marble!" I shouted. "I *need* marble."

It was my home and my nest. It was fucking beautiful. But I think I knew then that I'd become weird.

I'd had these two kids back-to-back. My hormones were all over the place. I was meaner than hell and so bossy. It was such a big deal for me to have kids. In trying to make our home perfect, I had gone over the top. I look back now and think, *God, that was bad*. I'm sorry, contractors. I think I cared too much.

I had an artist come in and paint murals in the boys' rooms: fantastical paintings of little boys on the moon. I just went all out.

It was my dream to have children and raise them in the coziest environment I could create. To me they were perfect, beautiful, everything I'd ever wanted. I wanted to give them the world—the whole solar system.

I began to suspect that I was a bit overprotective when I wouldn't let my mom hold Jayden for the first two months. Even after that, I'd let her hold him for five minutes and that was it. I had to have him back in my arms. That's too much. I know that now. I shouldn't have been that controlling.

Again, I think what happened when I first saw them after they'd been born was similar to what happened to me after the breakup with Justin: It was that *Benjamin Button* thing. I aged backward. Honestly, as a new mother, it was as if some part of me became the baby. One part of me was a very demanding grown woman yelling about white marble, while another part of me was suddenly very childlike.

Kids are so healing in one way. They make you less judgmental. Here they are, so innocent and so dependent on you.

You realize everyone was a baby once, so fragile and so helpless. In another way, for me, having kids was psychologically very complicated. It had happened when Jamie Lynn was born, too. I loved her so much and was so empathic that I became her in this strange way. When she was three, some part of me became three, too.

I've heard that this sometimes happens to parents—especially if you have trauma from your childhood. When your kids get to be the age you were when you were dealing with something rough, you relive it emotionally.

Unfortunately, there wasn't the same conversation about mental health back then that there is now. I hope any new mothers reading this who are having a hard time will get help early and will channel their feelings into something more healing than white marble floors. Because I now know that I was displaying just about every symptom of perinatal depression: sadness, anxiety, fatigue. Once the babies were born, I added on my confusion and obsession about the babies' safety, which was ratcheting up the more media attention was on us. Being a new mom is challenging enough without trying to do everything under a microscope.

With Kevin away so much, no one was around to see me spiral—except every paparazzo in America.

22

Those first few months after Jayden came home were a blur. I got a dog. Felicia came in and out of my life.

While I was pregnant with Jayden, I'd dyed my hair black. Trying to get it blond again, I turned it purple. I had to go to a beauty salon to have them completely strip my hair and make it a realistic shade of brown. It took forever to get it right. Nearly everything in my life felt like that. To say the least, there was some chaos: the breakup with J and going on the rough Onyx tour, marrying someone who no one seemed to think was a good match, and then trying to be a good mother inside of a marriage that was collapsing in real time.

And yet, I always felt so happy and creative in the studio. Recording for *Blackout*, I felt so much freedom. Working with amazing producers, I got to play. A producer named Nate Hills, who recorded under the name Danja, was more into dance and EDM than pop; he introduced me to new sounds and I got to stretch my voice in different ways.

I loved that no one was overthinking things and that I got to say what I liked and didn't like. I knew exactly what I wanted, and I loved so much of what was offered to me. Coming into the studio and hearing these incredible sounds and getting to put down a vocal on them was fun. Despite my reputation at the time, I was focused and excited to work when I came in. It was what was going on outside the studio that was so upsetting.

The paparazzi were like an army of zombies trying to get in every second. They tried to scale the walls and take pictures through windows. Trying to enter and exit a building felt like being part of a military operation. It was terrifying.

My A&R rep, Teresa LaBarbera Whites, who was a mother, too, did what she could to help. She put a baby swing at one of our studios, which I thought was a really sweet gesture.

The album was a kind of battle cry. After years of being meticulous, trying to please my mom and my dad, it was my time to say "Fuck you." I quit doing business the way I always had before. I started doing videos on the street myself. I would go into bars with a friend, and the friend would just bring a camera, and that's how we shot "Gimme More."

To be clear, I'm not saying I'm proud of it. "Gimme More" is by far the worst video I've ever shot in my life. I don't like it at all—it's so tacky. It looks like we only spent three thousand dollars to shoot it. And yet, even though it was bad, it worked for what it was. And the more I started going and doing things myself, the more interesting people started noticing and wanting to work with me. I wound up randomly finding really good people, just by word of mouth.

Blackout was one of the easiest and most satisfying albums I ever made. It came together really fast. I would go into the studio, be in there for thirty minutes, and leave. That wasn't by design—it had to be fast. If I stayed in one place for too long, the paparazzi outside would multiply like I was a cornered Pac-Man being chased by ghosts. My survival mechanism was to get in and get out of studios as fast as possible.

When I recorded "Hot as Ice," I walked into the studio and there were six gigantic guys in the room with me, sitting there. That was probably one of the most spiritual recording moments of my life, being with all those guys quietly listening as I sang. My voice went the highest it had ever gone. I sang it two times through and left. I didn't even have to try.

If making *Blackout* felt good, life was still tearing at me from every different direction. From one minute to the next, everything was so extreme. I needed to have more self-worth and value than I was able to conjure back then. And yet, even though it was a very hard time in just about every other way, artistically it was great. Something about where I was in my head made me a better artist.

I felt an exciting rush making the *Blackout* album. I was able to work in the best studios. It was a wild time.

Unfortunately, when family life is bad, that takes over and makes anything good on the other side feel less good. I mourn how unpleasant things got for me with my family, yet I remain so proud of that album. Many artists have said that it influenced them, and I often hear from fans that it's their favorite.

Meanwhile, Kevin was doing a lot of press, and you would've thought he'd just hit a grand slam in the World Series. I didn't know who he was anymore. Then he was asked to do a Super Bowl commercial for Nationwide. It didn't matter that the ad was him making fun of himself—playing a fast-food worker who dreams of being a star. After he got that offer, I basically never saw him. It was like he was too good to even talk to me. He told everyone else that being a father was everything to him—the best thing in his life. You wouldn't know it. Because the sad truth was, he was away a lot.

23

When I married Kevin, I meant it with all my heart. If you look into my eyes in my wedding photos, you can see it: I was so in love and so ready for a new phase of my life to start. I wanted babies with this man. I wanted a cozy home. I wanted to grow old with him.

My lawyer told me that if I didn't file for divorce, Kevin would. What I gathered from this was that Kevin wanted to file for divorce but he felt guilty doing it. He knew that it would make him look better publicly if I was the one who filed. My lawyer told me that Kevin was going to file for divorce no matter what. I was led to believe that it would be better if I did it first so that I wasn't humiliated.

I didn't want to be embarrassed, so in early November 2006, when Jayden was almost two months old, I filed the papers. Kevin and I both asked for full custody of the boys. What I did not understand was that Kevin would then insist I pay for his legal bills. And because legally, I had set the divorce in motion, I would be held responsible in the press for having broken up my young family.

The media attention was crazy. It was probably good for Kevin's album, which came out a week before we announced our divorce, but I was vilified. Some people tried to be supportive—but in the press, they often did this by being cruel toward Kevin, which actually wasn't that helpful.

Later that month, I presented at the American Music Awards. As I waited to go out onstage, Jimmy Kimmel delivered a monologue and skit about Kevin, who he called "the world's first-ever no-hit wonder." They sealed a stand-in into a crate and put it on a truck and dumped it into the ocean.

But this was the father of my two infant sons. I found the violence toward him unsettling. The whole audience was laughing. I hadn't known that was going to happen and it caught me completely off guard. I went out onstage and gave the award to Mary J. Blige, but I went backstage afterward and tried to make it clear that I had been blindsided and didn't like it. I also didn't think that in the midst of a custody battle, having my ex-husband treated that way would be of any benefit to me.

Everyone seemed to be delighted by news of our divorce— everyone except me. I did not feel like celebrating.

*   *   *

Looking back, I think that both Justin and Kevin were very clever. They knew what they were doing, and I played right into it.

That's the thing about this industry. I never knew how to play the game. I didn't know how to present myself on any level. I was a bad dresser—hell, I'm still a bad dresser, and I'll admit that. And I work on that. I try. But as much as I'll own my flaws, ultimately, I know that I am a good person. I can see now that you have to be smart enough, vicious enough, deliberate enough to play the game, and I did not know the game. I was truly innocent—just clueless. I was a newly single mom of two little boys—I didn't have the time to fix my hair before I went out into a sea of photographers.

So I was young, and I made a lot of mistakes. But I will say this: I wasn't manipulative. I was just stupid.

That's one thing Justin and Kevin ruined about me. I used to trust people. But after the breakup with Justin and then my divorce, I never really did trust people again.

24

One of the people who was kindest to me when I really needed kindness was Paris Hilton. So much of America dismissed her as a party girl, but I found her elegant—the way she posed on the red carpet and always had an arched eyebrow when anyone was mean about her.

She saw that I had babies and that I was suffering from the breakup, and I think she felt sorry for me. She came over to my house, and she helped me out so much. She was just so *sweet* to me. Aside from that night in Vegas with Jason Trawick, it felt like no one had been sweet like that to me in ages. We started hanging out. She encouraged me to try to have fun for the first time in a long time.

With Paris, I went through my party stage. But let's be clear: it was never as wild as the press made it out to be. There was a time when I never went out at all. Finally, when—with the kids properly supervised at home by capable caregivers—I did leave home for a few hours, stayed out late, and drank like any other twentysomething, I heard nothing but that I was the worst mother who'd ever lived and a terrible person, too. The tabloids were full of accusations: *She's a slut! She's on drugs!*

I never had a drinking problem. I liked to drink, but it was never out of control. Do you want to know my drug of choice? The only thing I really did except for drinking? Adderall, the amphetamine that's given to kids for ADHD. Adderall made me high, yes, but what I found far more appealing was that it gave me a few hours of feeling less depressed. It was the only thing that worked for me as an antidepressant, and I really felt like I needed one of those.

I have never had any interest in hard drugs. I saw plenty of people in the music world doing all that, but it wasn't for me. Where I grew up, what we did more than anything was drink beer; to this day, I don't like to drink expensive wine because it burns my throat. And I've never even liked weed except for that one time in New York when I broke my heel. If I just get a contact high from being around it, it makes me feel slow and dumb. I hate it.

Do you know what Paris and I did that supposedly crazy night everyone made such a big deal about, when we went out with Lindsay Lohan? We got drunk. That's it!

We were staying at a beach house and my mom was taking care of the kids, so I went out with Paris. We were hyped up, drinking and being silly. It felt good to be with friends and to cut loose. There wasn't one thing about it that felt wrong.

At the end of one night, I walked into the beach house, happy from my adventure and still a little drunk.

My mother was waiting up. When I walked in, she screamed at me and we got into a huge fight.

She said it was because I was wasted.

She wasn't wrong. I absolutely was. But that wasn't a violation of some cardinal rule in our family. And on that night, I'd had her babysit so I could go out responsibly, without the kids seeing their mother under the influence.

The shame I felt killed my heart. I stood there, reeling, and thought, *Okay. I guess it's forbidden for me to party.*

My mom always made me feel like I was bad or guilty of something, even though I had worked so hard to be good. That's what my family has always done—treated me like I was bad. The fight marked a turning point in my relationship with my mom. I couldn't go back to the way it was before. We tried, but it didn't really work.

No matter how many fans I had in the world, my parents never seemed to think I was worth much. How could you treat your child like that when she was going through a divorce, when she was lonely and lost?

Giving a person no grace in a hard time is just not nice, especially when you can't take as good as you give. When I started to speak up and throw it back at them a little—God knows they were far from perfect—they didn't really like it that much. But they still held so much emotional power over me.

25

Everything everyone says about becoming a parent was true for me. My boys gave my life meaning. I was shocked by how much pure and instant love I felt for those tiny creatures.

And yet, becoming a mother while under so much pressure at home and out in the world was also much, much harder than I expected it would be.

Cut off from my friends, I started to get weird. I know you're supposed to focus only on being a mother at those times, but it was hard for me to sit down and play with them each day, to put being a mother first. I felt so confused. All I had known my whole life was being exposed on every level. I didn't know where to go or what to do. Was I supposed to go home to Louisiana, get a house with a wall around it, and hide?

What I can see now but couldn't see then is that every part of normal life had been stripped from me—going out in public without becoming a headline, making normal mistakes as a new mother of two babies, feeling like I could trust the people around me. I had no freedom and yet also no security. At the same time I was also suffering, I now know, from severe postpartum depression. I'll admit it, I felt that I couldn't live if things didn't get better.

All these other people were doing their thing, but I was being watched from every corner. Justin and Kevin were able to have all the sex and smoke all the weed in the world and no one said one word to them. I came home from a night at the clubs and my own mother tore into me. It made me scared to do anything. My family made me feel paralyzed.

I gravitated toward anyone who would step in and act as a buffer between me and them, especially people who would take me out partying and get me temporarily distracted from all the surveillance I was under. Not all of these people were great in the long run, but at the time I was desperate for anyone who seemed to want to help me in any way and who seemed like they had the ability to keep my parents at bay.

As part of his bid for full custody, Kevin tried to convince everyone that I was completely out of control. He started to say I shouldn't have my kids anymore—at all.

When he said that, I remember thinking in my head, *Surely, this is a joke. This is just for the tabloids.* When you read about married celebrities fighting, you never really know what's real. I always assume that a lot of what you hear are stories being fed to the papers as part of some ploy to get the upper hand in a custody battle. So I kept waiting for him to bring the boys back to me after he took them. He not only wouldn't bring them back to me, he wouldn't let me *see* them for weeks on end.

In January 2007, my aunt Sandra died after a long and brutal struggle with ovarian cancer. She was like my second mother. By Aunt Sandra's grave at the funeral, I cried harder than I ever had.

Working felt unthinkable to me. A popular director called me during that time about a project he was working on. "I have a role for you to play," he said. "It's a really dark role."

I said no because I thought it wouldn't be emotionally healthy for me. But I wonder if just knowing about the part, subconsciously I went there in my head—imagined what it would be like to be her.

On the inside, I'd felt a cloud of darkness for a long time. On the outside, though, I'd tried to keep looking the way people wanted me to, keep acting the way they wanted me to—sweet and pretty all the time. But the veneer had been so worn away by this point that there was nothing left. I was a raw nerve.

*   *   *

In February, after not getting to see the boys for weeks and weeks, completely beside myself with grief, I went to plead to see them. Kevin wouldn't let me in. I begged him. Jayden James was five months old and Sean Preston was seventeen months old. I imagined their not knowing where their mother was, wondering why she didn't want to be with them. I wanted to get a battering ram to get to them. I didn't know what to do.

The paparazzi watched it all happen. I can't describe the humiliation I felt. I was cornered. I was out being chased, like always, by these men waiting for me to do something they could photograph.

And so that night I gave them some material.

I went into a hair salon, and I took the clippers, and I shaved off all my hair.

Everyone thought it was hilarious. *Look how crazy she is!* Even my parents acted embarrassed by me. But nobody seemed to understand that I was simply out of my mind with grief. My children had been taken away from me.

With my head shaved, everyone was scared of me, even my mom. No one would talk to me anymore because I was too ugly.

My long hair was a big part of what people liked—I knew that. I knew a lot of guys thought long hair was hot.

Shaving my head was a way of saying to the world: *Fuck you.*

You want me to be pretty for you? Fuck you. You want me to be good for you? Fuck you. You want me to be your dream girl? Fuck you. I'd been the good girl for years. I'd smiled politely while TV show hosts leered at my breasts, while American parents said I was destroying their children by wearing a crop top, while executives patted my hand condescendingly and second-guessed my career choices even though I'd sold millions of records, while my family acted like I was evil. And I was tired of it.

At the end of the day, I didn't care. All I wanted to do was see my boys. It made me sick thinking about the hours, the days, the weeks I missed with them. My most special moments in life were taking naps with my children. That's the closest I've ever felt to God—taking naps with my precious babies, smelling their hair, holding their tiny hands.

I became incredibly angry. I think a lot of other women understand this. A friend of mine once said: "If someone took my baby away from me, I would have done a lot more than get a haircut. I would have burned the city to the ground."

26

Flailing those weeks without my children, I lost it, over and over again. I didn't even really know how to take care of myself. Because of the divorce, I'd had to move out of the home I loved and was living in a random English-style cottage in Beverly Hills. The paparazzi were circling extra-excitedly now, like sharks when there's blood in the water.

When I first shaved my head, it felt almost religious. I was living on a level of pure *being*.

For when I wanted to go out into the world, I bought seven wigs, all short bobs. But if I couldn't see my sons, I didn't want to see anybody.

A few days after I shaved my head, my cousin Alli drove me back to Kevin's. At least I'd thought there'd be no paparazzi to see it this time. But apparently someone tipped one of the photographers off, and he called his buddy.

When we stopped at a gas station, the pair of them came for me. They kept taking flash pictures with a giant camera and videotaping me through the window as I sat, heartbroken, in the passenger seat, waiting for Alli to come back. One of them was asking questions: "How are you doing? You doing okay? I'm concerned about you."

We drove on to Kevin's. The two paparazzi kept following us, taking pictures as I was, once again, denied entry to Kevin's. Turned away, trying to see my own children.

After we left, Alli pulled over so we could figure out what to do next. The videographer was right there at my window again.

"What I'm going to do, Britney—all I'm going to do—is I'm going to ask you a few questions," one of them said with that mean look on his face. He wasn't asking if he could. He was telling me what he was going to do to me. "And then I'm going to leave you alone."

Alli started begging the men to go away. "Please, guys. Don't, guys. Please, please . . ."

She was being so polite, and she was pleading with them as if she was asking them to spare our lives, which it sort of felt like she was.

But they wouldn't stop. I screamed.

They liked that—when I reacted. One guy wouldn't go away until he got what he wanted. He kept smirking, kept asking me the same terrible questions, over and over, trying to get me to react again. There was so much ugliness in his voice—such a lack of humanity.

This was one of the worst moments of my whole life, and he kept after me. Couldn't he treat me like a human being? Couldn't he back off? But he wouldn't. He just kept coming. He kept asking me, over and over again, how I felt not being able to see my kids. He was smiling.

Finally, I snapped.

I grabbed the only thing within reach, a green umbrella, and jumped out of the car. I wasn't going to hit him, because even at my worst, I am not that kind of person. I hit the next closest thing, which was his car.

Pathetic, really. An umbrella. You can't even do any damage with an umbrella. It was a desperate move by a desperate person.

I was so embarrassed by what I'd done that I sent the photo agency an apology note, mentioning that I'd been in the running for a dark film role, which was true, and that I wasn't quite myself, which was also true.

Later, that paparazzo would say in an interview for a documentary about me, "That was not a good night for her . . . But it *was* a good night for us—'cause we got the money shot."

*   *   *

Now my husband, Hesam, tells me that it's a whole thing for beautiful girls to shave their heads. It's a vibe, he says—a choice not to play into ideas of conventional beauty. He tries to make me feel better about it, because he feels bad about how much it still pains me.

27

It felt like I was living on the edge of a cliff.

Sometime after I shaved my head, I went to Bryan's apartment in Los Angeles. He had two girlfriends from his past in Mississippi with him—my mom was there, too. It was like my mom wouldn't even look at me because I was ugly now. It just proved that the world only cares about your physical appearance, even if you are suffering and at your lowest point.

That winter, I'd been told it would help me get custody back if I went to rehab. And so, even though I felt I had more of a rage and grief problem than a substance abuse problem, I went. When I arrived, my father was there. He sat across from me—there were three picnic tables between us. He said, "You are a disgrace."

I look back now and I think, *Why didn't I call Big Rob to help me?* I was so ashamed and embarrassed already, but here was my dad telling me I was a disgrace. It was the definition of beating a dead horse. He was treating me like a dog, an ugly dog. I had nobody. I was so alone. I guess one positive of rehab was that I started the healing process. I was determined to make the best of a dark situation.

When I got out, I was able to get temporary fifty-fifty custody through a great attorney who helped me. But the battle kept raging with Kevin and it was eating me alive.

Blackout, the thing I'm most proud of in my whole career, came out right around Halloween in 2007. I was supposed to perform "Gimme More" at the VMAs to help promote it. I didn't want to, but my team was pressuring me to get out there and show the world I was fine.

The only problem with this plan: I was not fine.

Backstage at the VMAs that night, nothing was going right. There was a problem with my costume and with my hair extensions. I hadn't slept the night before. I was dizzy. It was less than a year since I'd had my second baby in two years but everyone was acting like my not having six-pack abs was offensive. I couldn't believe I was going to have to go out onstage feeling the way I felt.

I ran into Justin backstage. It had been a while since I'd seen him. Everything was going great in his world. He was at the top of his game in every way, and he had a lot of swagger.

I was having a panic attack. I hadn't rehearsed enough. I hated the way I looked. I knew it was going to be bad.

I went out there and did the best I could at that moment in time, which—yes, granted—was far from my best at other times. I could see myself on video throughout the auditorium while I performed; it was like looking at myself in a fun-house mirror.

I'm not going to defend that performance or say it was good, but I will say that as performers we all have bad nights. They don't usually have consequences so extreme.

You also don't usually have one of the worst days of your life in the same exact place and time that your ex has one of his best.

Justin glided down the runway into his performance. He was flirting with girls in the audience, including one who turned around and arched her back, shaking her breasts as he sang to her. Then he was sharing the stage with Nelly Furtado and Timbaland—so fun, so free, so light.

Later that night, the comedian Sarah Silverman came out onstage to roast me. She said that at the age of twenty-five I'd done everything worthwhile in my life I'd ever do. She called my two babies "the most adorable mistakes you'll ever see." I didn't hear that until later, though. At the time I was backstage sobbing hysterically.

In the days and weeks that followed, the newspapers made fun of my body and my performance. Dr. Phil called it a train wreck.

The only press I did for *Blackout* was a live radio inter-view with Ryan Seacrest when it came out in October 2007. In the interview, which was supposed to be about the record, Ryan Seacrest asked me questions like "How do you respond to those who criticize you as a mom?" and "Do you feel like you're doing everything you can for your kids?" and "How often will you see them?"

It felt like that was the only thing people wanted to talk about: whether or not I was a fit mother. Not about how I'd made such a strong album while holding two babies on my hips and being pursued by dozens of dangerous men all day every day.

My management team quit. A bodyguard went to court with Gloria Allred by his side as a witness in the custody case. He said I was doing drugs; he wasn't cross-examined.

A court-appointed parenting coach said that I loved my children and that we were clearly bonded. She also said that there was nothing at all in my home that could be called abuse.

But that part didn't make headlines.

28

One day in early January 2008, I had the boys, and at the end of the visit a security guard who used to work for me and now worked for Kevin came to pick them up.

First he put Preston in the car. When he came to get Jayden, the thought hit me: *I may never see my boys again*. Given how things had been going with my custody case, I'd become terrified that I wouldn't get the kids again if I gave them back.

I ran into the bathroom with Jayden and locked the door—I just couldn't let him go. I didn't want anyone taking my baby. A friend was there and came to the bathroom door and told me the security guard would wait. I held Jayden and cried so hard. But no one was giving me extra time. Before I knew what was happening, a SWAT team in black suits burst through the bathroom door as if I'd hurt someone. The only thing I was guilty of was feeling desperate to keep my own children for a few more hours and to get some assurance that I wasn't going to lose them for good. I looked at my friend and just said, "But you said he would wait . . ."

Once they'd taken Jayden from me, they tied me onto a gurney and took me to the hospital.

The hospital let me go before the end of a seventy-two-hour hold. But the damage was already done. And it didn't help that the paparazzi were getting worse in their hounding of me.

A new custody hearing was held and I was told that now—because I'd been so scared to lose the kids that I'd panicked—I would be allowed to see them even less.

I felt like no one had my back. Even my family seemed not to care. Right around the holidays, I found out about my sixteen-year-old sister's pregnancy from an exclusive in the tabloids. The family had kept it from me. This was around the time that Jamie Lynn almost filed for emancipation from our parents. Among the things she has accused them of was taking away her cell phone. She wound up having to talk to the outside world through burner phones she kept secret.

I now see that if someone's not doing well—and I was really not doing well—that's the time you need to come to that person and hold them. Kevin took my world away from me. He knocked the breath out of me. And my family did not hold me.

I began to suspect that they were secretly celebrating that I was having the worst time in my life. But surely that couldn't be the case, right? Surely I was paranoid.

Right?

29

Los Angeles is warm and sunny all year round. Driving through the city, sometimes it's hard to remember what season it is. Everywhere you look, people are wearing sunglasses and drinking cold drinks out of straws, smiling and laughing underneath the clear blue sky. But in January 2008, winter really felt like winter, even in California, because I felt alone and cold and I was hospitalized.

I probably shouldn't admit to this, but I was hell on wheels. I was taking a lot of Adderall.

I was horrible, and I will admit to doing wrong. I was so angry about what happened with Kevin. I'd tried so hard with him. I'd given my everything.

And he'd turned on me.

I had started dating a photographer. I was completely infatuated with him. He'd been a paparazzo, and I understood that people thought he was up to no good, but all I could see at the time was that he was chivalrous and helped me out when the others got too aggressive.

Back then I would speak up if I didn't like something—I would certainly let you know. And I wouldn't think twice about it. (If I had been hit in the face in Vegas—as happened to me in July 2023—I would've hit the person back, 100 percent.)

I was fearless.

We were always being chased by the paparazzi. The chases were really insane—sometimes they were aggressive, and sometimes they were playful, too. Many of the paps were trying to make me look bad, to get the money shot to show "Oh, she's lost and she looks crazy right now." But sometimes they wanted me to look good, too.

One day, the photographer and I were being chased, and this was one of those moments with him that I'll never forget. We were driving fast, near the edge of a cliff, and I don't know why, but I decided to pull a 360, right there on the edge. I honestly didn't even know I could do a 360—it was completely beyond me, so I think it was God. But I stuck it; the back wheels of the car stopped on what seemed like the very edge, and if the wheels had rotated maybe three more times, we would have just gone off the cliff.

I looked at him; he looked at me.

"We could have just died," I said.

I felt so alive.

As parents we're always telling our children, "Stay safe. Don't do this; don't do that." But even though safety is the most important thing, I also think it's important to have awakenings and challenge ourselves to feel liberated, to be fearless and experience everything the world has to offer.

I didn't know then that the photographer was married; I had no clue that I was essentially his mistress. I only found that out after we'd broken up. I'd just thought he was a lot of fun and our time together was incredibly hot. He was ten years older than me.

Everywhere I went—and for a while I went out a lot— the paparazzi were there. And yet, for all the reports about my being out of control, I don't know that I was ever out of control in a way that warranted what came next. The truth is that I was *sad*, beyond sad, missing my kids when they were with Kevin.

The photographer helped me with my depression. I longed for attention, and he gave me the attention I needed. It was just a lustful relationship. My family didn't like him, but there was a lot about them I didn't like, either.

The photographer encouraged me to rebel. He let me sow my oats and he still loved me for it. He loved me unconditionally. It wasn't like my mom screaming at me for partying. He said, "Girl, go, you got it, do your thing!" He wasn't like my father, who set impossible conditions for his love.

And so, with the photographer's support, I 100 percent did my thing. And it felt radical to be that wild. That far from what everyone wanted me to be.

I talked as if I were out of my mind. I was so loud—everywhere I went, even at restaurants. People would go out to eat with me, and I would lie down on the table. It was a way of saying "Fuck you!" to any person who came my way.

I mean, I will say it: I was *bad*.

Or maybe I wasn't bad so much as very, very angry.

I wanted to escape. I didn't have my kids, and I needed to get away from the media and the paparazzi. I wanted to leave LA, so the photographer and I went on a trip to Mexico.

It was like I'd fled to a safe house. Everywhere else there'd be a million people outside my door. But when I left LA, even though it was for a short time, I felt far from everything. This worked—I felt better for a little while. I should have taken more advantage of it.

It seemed like my relationship with the photographer was getting more serious, and as that happened, I sensed that my family was trying to get closer to me—in a way that made me uneasy.

My mom called me one day and said, "Britney, we feel like something's going on. We hear that the cops are after you. Let's go to the beach house."

"The cops are after me?" I said. "For what?" I hadn't done

anything illegal. That I knew for sure. I'd had my moments. I'd had my wild spell. I'd been high on Adderall and acted crazy. But I didn't do anything criminal. In fact, as she knew, I'd been with girlfriends the prior two days. My mom and I had had a sleepover with my cousin Alli and two other girlfriends.

"Just come to the house!" she said. "We want to talk to you."

So I went to the house with them. The photographer met me there.

My mother was acting suspicious.

When the photographer got there, he said, "Something's up, right?"

"Yeah," I said. "Something's really off." All of a sudden, there were helicopters going around the house.

"Is that for me?" I asked my mom. "Is this a joke?"

It wasn't a joke.

Suddenly there was a SWAT team of what seemed like twenty cops in my house.

"What the fuck did I do?" I kept shouting. "I didn't do anything!"

I know I had been acting wild but there was nothing I'd done that justified their treating me like I was a bank robber. Nothing that justified upending my entire life.

I'd later come to believe something had changed that month, since the last time I was brought to the hospital for evaluation.

My father had struck up a very close friendship with Louise "Lou" Taylor, who he worshipped. She was front and center during the implementation of the conservatorship that would later allow them to control and take over my career. Lou, who had just started a new company called Tri Star Sports & Entertainment Group, was directly involved in calling the shots right before the conservatorship. At the time, she had few real clients. She basically used my name and hard work to build her company.

Conservatorships, also called guardianships, are usually reserved for people with no mental capacity, people who can't do anything for themselves. But I was highly functional. I'd just done the best album of my career. I was making a lot of people a lot of money, especially my father, who I found out took a bigger salary than he paid me. He paid himself more than $6 million while paying others close to him tens of millions more.

The thing is, you can have a conservatorship that lasts for two months and then the person gets on track and you let them control their life again, but that wasn't what my father wanted. He wanted far more.

My dad was able to set up two forms of conservatorship: what's called "conservatorship of the person" and "conservatorship of the estate." The conservator of the person is designated to control details of the conservatee's life, like where they live, what they eat, whether they can drive a car, and what they do day-to-day. Even though I begged the court to appoint *literally anyone else*—and I mean, anyone off the street would have been better—my father was given the job, the same man who'd made me cry if I had to get in the car with him when I was a little girl because he talked to himself. And the court was told that I was demented, and I wasn't even allowed to pick my own lawyer.

The conservator of the estate—an estate worth, in my case, tens of millions of dollars at one point—manages the conservatee's affairs to keep them from being "subject to undue influence or fraud." This role was taken by my father in conjunction with a lawyer named Andrew Wallet, who would eventually be paid $426,000 a year for keeping me from my own money. I would be forced to pay upward of $500,000 a year to my court-appointed lawyer, who I wasn't allowed to replace.

It felt like my father and Lou's employee Robin Greenhill ruled my life and monitored every move I made. I'm a five-foot-four-inch pop singer who calls everyone "sir" and "ma'am." They treated me like I was a criminal or predator.

There were times when I needed my father over the years and I reached out, and he wasn't there. But when it came time for him to be the conservator, of course he was on the case! He's always been all about the money.

I can't say my mom was that much better. She'd acted innocent while she was there for two sleepover nights with my girlfriends and me. She'd known the whole time that they were going to take me away. I am convinced that it was all planned and that my dad and my mom and Lou Taylor were all involved. Tri Star was even planning to be my co-conservator. Later, I learned that at the time they put me into the conservatorship, on the heels of his bankruptcy, my dad had been financially indebted to Lou, owing her at least $40,000, a lot for him, especially back then. That is what my new lawyer Mathew Rosengart later called a "conflict of interest" in court.

Soon after I was brought to the hospital against my will, I was informed that the conservatorship papers had been filed.

30

As everything was falling apart for me, my mother was writing a memoir. She wrote about watching her beautiful daughter shaving off her hair and wondering how that was possible. She said that I used to be "the happiest little girl in the world."

When I made the wrong move, it was like my mother wasn't concerned. She would share my every mistake on television, promoting her book.

She wrote it trading on my name and talking about her parenting of me and my brother and sister at a time when all three of us kids were basket cases. Jamie Lynn was a pregnant teenager. Bryan was struggling to find his place in the world and still convinced he was letting our father down. And I was in full meltdown.

When the book came out, she appeared on every morning show to promote it. I would turn on the TV to see B-roll of my videos and my shaved head flashing on the screen. My mother was telling Meredith Vieira on the *Today* show that she'd spent hours wondering how things went so wrong with me. On another show, the audience clapped when she said my sister was pregnant at sixteen. That was classy as shit, apparently, because she was still with the father! Yes, how wonderful—she was married to her husband and having a baby at seventeen. *They're still together! Great! It doesn't matter that she's a child having a child!*

I was in one of the darkest times in my life, and my mom was telling the audience, "Oh yeah, and here's . . . Britney."

And every show was plastering images of me with my shaved head on the screen.

The book was huge for her, and all at my expense. The timing was un-fucking-believable.

I am willing to admit that in the throes of severe postpartum depression, abandonment by my husband, the torture of being separated from my two babies, the death of my adored aunt Sandra, and the constant drumbeat of pressure from paparazzi, I'd begun to think in some ways like a child.

And yet I look at the worst things I did during that time and I don't believe the sum total of them is anywhere near as cruel as what my mother did by writing and promoting that book.

She was on morning talk shows trying to sell her book about when I was in hospitals and being driven insane because

I was separated from my babies for weeks on end. She was making money off that dark time.

In those days, I wasn't the brightest bulb on the tree. It's the truth. But what plenty of people took away from my mother's book was: "Oh, Britney's so bad." Her book even made *me* believe I was bad! And she did it at a time when I already felt so much shame.

I swear to God, it makes me want to cry to think about my kids going through anything hard like I was going through when they were babies. If one of my sons were going through something like that, do you think I would write a book about it?

I would fall to my knees. I would do anything I could to help him through it, to hold him, to make it better.

The last thing I would do would be to cut my hair into a bob and put on a tasteful pantsuit and sit down on a morning-show set across from Meredith fucking Vieira and make money off my child's misfortune.

Sometimes I talk trash on Instagram. People don't know why I have such anger toward my parents. But I think if they were in my shoes, they would understand.

31

The conservatorship was created supposedly because I was incapable of doing anything at all—feeding myself, spending my own money, being a mother, anything. So why was it that a few weeks later, they had me shoot an episode of *How I Met Your Mother* and then sent me on a grueling world tour?

After the conservatorship started, my mom and my brother's girlfriend got short haircuts and went out to dinner drinking wine—paparazzi were there, taking their picture. It all felt set up. My dad took my boyfriend away and I could not drive. My mom and dad took my womanhood from me. It was a win-win for them.

I remained shocked that the state of California would let a man like my father—an alcoholic, someone who'd declared bankruptcy, who'd failed in business, who'd terrified me as a little girl—control me after all my accomplishments and everything I had done.

I thought about advice my father had given me over the years that I'd resisted, and I wondered if I'd be able to resist anymore. My father presented the conservatorship as a great stepping stone on the road to my "comeback." Just months earlier I'd released the best album of my career, but fine. What I heard in what my father said was: "She's great now! She's working for us! It's a perfect situation for our family."

Was it great for *me*? Or was it great for *him*?

How fun! I thought. *I can go back to working again like nothing at all happened! Too sick to choose my own boyfriend and yet somehow healthy enough to appear on sitcoms and morning shows, and to perform for thousands of people in a different part of the world every week!*

From that point on, I began to think that he saw me as put on the earth for no other reason than to help their cash flow.

At my house, my father took over my little study and my bar area and turned it into his office. There was a bowl there that had a bunch of receipts in it.

Yes, here's my confession: I was so nerdy that I kept all my receipts in a bowl. Each week, I would add up my expenses old-school style to keep track of my deductions for taxes. Even when I was going through a wild spell, the fundamentals of who I was as a person were still there. To me, that bowl of receipts was proof that I was still capable of managing my affairs.

I knew musicians who did heroin, got in fistfights, and threw TVs out of hotel windows. Not only didn't I steal anything or hurt anyone or do hard drugs—*I was keeping track of my tax deductions.*

Not anymore. My father shoved aside my bowl of receipts, setting up his things on the bar. "I just want to let you know," he said, "I call the shots. You sit right there in that chair and I'll tell you what goes on."

I looked at him with a growing sense of horror.

"I'm Britney Spears now," he said.

32

On the rare occasion that I went out—like to my agent and friend Cade's house for a dinner party—the security team would sweep through the house before I arrived to make sure there was no alcohol or any drugs, even Tylenol, there. No one at the party was allowed to drink until I left. The other guests were all very good sports about it, but I sensed that the second I left was when the real party started.

When someone wanted to date me, the security team who answered to my father would run a background check on him, make him sign an NDA, and even have him submit to a blood test. (And my father said I couldn't see the photographer I had been dating ever again, too.)

Before a date, Robin would tell the man my medical and sexual history. To be clear: this was before the first date. The whole thing was humiliating, and I know the insanity of this system kept me from finding basic companionship, having a fun night out, or making new friends—let alone falling in love.

Thinking back on the way my father was raised by June and the way I was brought up by him, I had known from the jump that it would be an actual nightmare to have him in charge. The thought of my father taking over any aspect of my life had filled me with fear. But taking over everything? It was just the worst thing that could possibly ever happen to my music, my career, and my sanity.

Pretty quickly, I called the weird-ass lawyer the court had appointed for me and asked him for help. Incredibly, he was all I really had—even though I hadn't chosen him. I had been told that I couldn't hire anyone new, because my lawyer had to be court-approved. Much later, I would come to find out that was bullshit: I didn't know for thirteen years that I could've gotten my own lawyer. I felt that the court-appointed lawyer didn't seem eager to help me understand what was going on, or to fight for my rights.

My mother, who is best friends with the governor of Louisiana, could have put me on the phone with him, and he would have told me I could get my own lawyer. But she kept it a secret; instead, she got a lawyer for herself just so she could get off on fighting with my dad, like she did when I was younger.

At various times I pushed back, especially when my father took away access to my cell phone. I would be smuggled a private phone and try to break free. But they always caught me.

And here's the sad, honest truth: after everything I had been through, I didn't have a lot of fight left in me. I was tired, and I was scared, too. After being held down on a gurney, I knew they could restrain my body any time they wanted to. *They could've tried to kill me*, I thought. I started to wonder if they did want to kill me.

So when my father said, "I call the shots," I thought, *This is too much for me.* But I didn't see a way out. So I felt my spirit retreat, and I went on autopilot. *If I play along, surely they'll see how good I am and they will let me go.*

And so I went along with it.

After I'd married Kevin and had my kids, Felicia was still there a little bit; I had always adored her, but once I stopped touring and started working less, we fell out of touch. There was some talk of Felicia's coming back on board for the Circus Tour, but somehow I never did have her as my assistant again. I later learned that my dad told her I didn't want her to work for me anymore. But I never said that. If I had known she wanted to do something for me, I never would have told her no. Without my knowledge, my father was keeping her from me.

I never saw some of my really close friends ever again—still haven't, to this day. It made me shut down psychologically even more than I had before.

My parents had some old friends from home come visit me to make me feel better.

"No, thanks," I said.

I mean, I loved them to death, but they had kids now, and they'd moved on with their lives. Their coming to see me felt more like sympathy than like a social call. Help is good, but not if it's not asked for. Not if it doesn't feel like it's a choice.

It's difficult for me to revisit this darkest chapter of my life and to think about what might have been different if I'd pushed back harder then. I don't at all like to think about that, not whatsoever. I can't afford to, honestly. I've been through too much.

And, when the conservatorship happened, it was true that I had been partying. My body couldn't physically take that anymore. It was time to calm down. But I went from partying a lot to being a total monk. Under the conservatorship, I didn't do anything.

One day I was with the photographer, driving my car fast, living so much. And then all of a sudden I was alone, doing nothing at all, not even always allowed access to my own cell phone. It was night and day.

In my old life I'd had freedom: the freedom to make my own decisions, to set my own agenda, to wake up and decide how I wanted to spend the day. Even the hard days were *my* hard days. Once I gave up the fight, in my new life, I would wake up each morning and ask one question: "What are we doing?"

And then I would do what I was told.

When I was alone at night, I would try to find inspiration in beautiful or transporting music, movies, books—anything to help blot out the horror of this arrangement. Just as I had when I was a little girl, I'd look for other worlds to escape into.

It seemed like every request went through my father and Robin. They decided where I went and with who. Under Robin's direction, security guards handed me prepackaged envelopes of meds and watched me take them. They put parental controls on my iPhone. Everything was scrutinized and controlled. Everything.

I would go to sleep early. And then I would wake up and do what they told me again. And again. And again. It was like *Groundhog Day*.

I did that for thirteen years.

If you're asking why I went along with it, there's one very good reason. I did it for my kids.

Because I played by the rules, I was reunited with my boys.

It was an ecstatic experience getting to hold them again. When they fell asleep next to me that first night we had back together, I felt whole for the first time in months. I just stared at them sleeping and felt so, so lucky.

To see them as much as possible, I did everything I could to appease Kevin. I paid his legal bills, plus child support, plus thousands more a month so the kids could come along with me on the Circus Tour. Within the same short period of time, I appeared on *Good Morning America*, did the Christmas-tree lighting in Los Angeles, shot a segment for *Ellen*, and toured through Europe and Australia. But again, the question was nagging at me—if I was so sick that I couldn't make my own decisions, why did they think it was fine for me to be out there smiling and waving and singing and dancing in a million time zones a week?

I'll tell you one good reason.

The Circus Tour grossed more than $130 million.

Lou Taylor's company, Tri Star, got 5 percent. And I learned, after the conservatorship, that even when I was on hiatus in 2019 and money wasn't coming in, my father paid them an extra minimum "flat fee," so they were paid hundreds of thousands of dollars more.

My father got a percentage, too, plus, throughout the conservatorship, about $16,000 a month, more than he'd ever made before. He profited heavily from the conservatorship, becoming a multimillionaire.

My freedom in exchange for naps with my children—
it was a trade I was willing to make. There is nothing I love
more—nothing more important to me on this earth—than my
children. I'd lay down my life for them.

So, I thought, *why not my freedom?*

33

How do you cling to hope? I had resolved to go along with the conservatorship for the sake of my sons, but being in it was *really hard*. I knew there was something more inside me, but I felt it dimming every day. Over time, the fire inside me burned out. The light went out of my eyes. I know that my fans could see it, although they didn't understand the full scope of what had happened, because I was so tightly controlled.

I have a lot of compassion for the woman I was before I was put into the conservatorship, when I was recording *Blackout*. Even though I was being described as so rebellious and such a wild girl, all my best work was accomplished during that time. All in all, though, it was a terrible time. I had my two little babies and there was always a fight around my trying to see them.

I look back now and I think that if I'd been wise, I

wouldn't have done anything but focus on my life at home, as hard as it was.

At the time Kevin would say, "Well, if you meet me this weekend, we'll have a two-hour meeting and we'll do this and that and I *might* let you see the boys a little bit more." Everything was almost like a deal with the devil for me to get what I wanted.

I was rebelling, yes, but I can see now that there's a reason why people go through rebellious times. And you have to let people go through them. I'm not saying that I was right to spiral, but I think to hinder someone's spirit to that degree and to put them down that much, to the point where they no longer feel like themselves—I don't think that's healthy, either. We, as people, have to test the world. You have to test your boundaries, to find out who you are, how you want to live.

Other people—and by *other people*, I mean men—were afforded that freedom. Male rockers were rolling in late to awards shows and we thought it made them cooler. Male pop stars were sleeping with lots of women and that was awesome. Kevin was leaving me alone with two babies when he wanted to go smoke pot and record a rap song, "Popozão," slang for *big ass* in Portuguese. Then he took them away from me, and he had *Details* magazine calling him Dad of the Year. A paparazzo who stalked and tormented me for months sued me for $230,000 for running over his foot with my car one time when I was trying to escape from him. We settled and I had to give him a lot of money.

When Justin cheated on me and then acted sexy, it was seen as cute. But when I wore a sparkly bodysuit, I had Diane Sawyer making me cry on national television, MTV making me listen to people criticizing my costumes, and a governor's wife saying she wanted to shoot me.

I'd been eyeballed so much growing up. I'd been looked up and down, had people telling me what they thought of my body, since I was a teenager. Shaving my head and acting out were my ways of pushing back. But under the conservatorship I was made to understand that those days were now over. I had to grow my hair out and get back into shape. I had to go to bed early and take whatever medication they told me to take.

If I thought getting criticized about my body in the press was bad, it hurt even more from my own father. He repeatedly told me I looked fat and that I was going to have to do something about it. So every day I would put on my sweats and I would go to the gym. I would do little bits of creative stuff here and there, but my heart wasn't in it anymore. As far as my passion for singing and dancing, it was almost a joke at that point.

Feeling like you're never good enough is a soul-crushing state of being for a child. He'd drummed that message into me as a girl, and even after I'd accomplished so much, he was continuing to do that to me.

You ruined me as a person, I wanted to tell my father. *Now you're making me work for you. I'll do it, but I'll be damned if I'll put my heart into it.*

I became a robot. But not just a robot—a sort of child-robot. I had been so infantilized that I was losing pieces of what made me feel like myself. Anything that my father or my mother told me to do, I would reject. My pride as a woman wouldn't let me take it seriously. The conservatorship stripped me of my womanhood, made me into a child. I became more of an entity than a person onstage. I had always felt music in my bones and my blood; they stole that from me.

If they'd let me live my life, I know I would've followed my heart and come out of this the right way and worked it out.

Thirteen years went by with me feeling like a shadow of myself. I think back now on my father and his associates having control over my body and my money for that long and it makes me feel sick.

Think of how many male artists gambled all their money away; how many had substance abuse or mental health issues. No one tried to take away *their control over their body and money*. I didn't deserve what my family did to me.

The thing was: I accomplished a lot during that time when I was supposedly incapable of taking care of myself.

In 2008, I won more than twenty awards, including a Cosmopolitan Ultimate Woman of the Year Award. At the VMAs, just one year after I'd been mocked for my "Gimme More" performance, I won three Moonmen. My video "Piece of Me" won every category it was nominated in, including Video of the Year. I thanked God, my sons, and my fans for standing by me.

I sometimes thought that it was almost funny how I won those awards for the album I made while I was supposedly so incapacitated that I had to be controlled by my family.

The truth was, though, when I stopped to think about it for very long, it wasn't funny at all.

34

While overall I was miserable, day-to-day I was able to find joy and comfort in the boys and in my routine. I made friends. I dated Jason Trawick. He was ten years older than me and really had his life together. I loved that he wasn't a performer but was an agent, so he knew the business and understood my life. We ended up dating for three years.

When we went out together, he was hypervigilant. I knew I could be clueless sometimes. (I'm not clueless anymore. Now I'm basically a CIA agent.) He was always scoping everything out, obsessively controlling situations. I'd been around the paparazzi so much that I knew what was up; I knew the deal. So to see him in a suit, working at this huge agency, getting in the car with me, I felt he was almost too aware of who I was. He cared too much about managing things. I was used to photographers swarming me on the streets and I hardly noticed them anymore, which I suppose isn't really good, either.

We did have a great relationship. I felt a lot of love for him and from him.

I was still messed up psychologically from everything that had happened with Kevin and my kids, and from living under the strictures of the conservatorship my father had set up. I had a place in Thousand Oaks, California. My kids were young at the time and my father was still in charge of my life.

Even though I was on a break after the Femme Fatale Tour, my father second-guessed every little thing I did, including what I ate. It puzzled me that my mom never said anything about it—my parents got back together in 2010, eight years after their divorce. And I felt so betrayed by the state of California. My mom seemed to love that because of the conservatorship, my dad now had a real job. They watched *Criminal Minds* on the couch every fucking night. Who does that?

When my father told me I couldn't have dessert, I felt that it was not just him telling me but my family and my state, like I was not allowed *legally* to eat dessert, because he said no.

Eventually, I started to ask myself, *Wait, where am I?* Nothing really made sense anymore.

Feeling like I needed more direction, I decided to go back to work. I tried to occupy myself by being productive. I began appearing on more TV shows—including, in 2012, as a judge on *The X Factor*.

I think a lot of people are really professional on TV, like Christina Aguilera and Gwen Stefani. When the camera is on them, they thrive. And that's great. I used to be able to do that when I was younger, but again, I feel like I age backward when I'm afraid. And so I got to where I was very, very nervous if I knew I had to be on air, and I didn't like being nervous all day long. Maybe I'm just not cut out for that anymore.

I've accepted that now, and it's okay. I can tell people who try to push me in that direction no. I've been forced into things I didn't want to do and been humiliated. It's not my thing at this point. Now, if you got me a cute cameo on a fun TV show where I'm in and out in a day, that's one thing, but to act skeptical for eight hours straight while judging people on TV? Uh, no thank you. I absolutely hated it.

It was around that time that I got engaged to Jason. He got me through a lot of things. But in 2012, not long after he became my co-conservator, my feelings changed. I couldn't see it then, but I see now that having him tied up with the organization controlling my life might have played a part in draining the romance out of our relationship. There came a point when I realized that I didn't have any bad feelings toward him, but I also didn't love him anymore. I stopped sleeping in the same room with him. I just wanted to cuddle my kids. I felt such a bond with them. I literally closed the door to him.

My mom said, "That is hateful."

"I'm sorry, I can't help it," I said. "I don't love him anymore like that."

He broke up with me, but I didn't care because I'd fallen out of love with him. He wrote me a long letter and then he disappeared. He resigned as my co-conservator when our relationship ended. To me it seemed that he had something of an identity crisis. He put colored streaks in his hair and went to the Santa Monica Pier and rode bikes every day with a bunch of tattooed dudes.

Hey, I get it. Now that I'm in my forties, I'm going through my own identity crisis. I think it was just time for us to part ways.

The tours under the conservatorship were strictly sober, so we weren't allowed to drink. Once, I ended up with most of the same dancers as Christina Aguilera. The dancers and I met up with Christina in Los Angeles. She seemed pretty messed up. But the dancers and I wound up swimming in a beautiful pool and sitting in a Jacuzzi. It would have been nice to have drinks with them, to get rebellious, sassy, fun. I wasn't allowed to do that because my life had become a Sunday-school Bible church camp under the conservatorship.

In some ways, they turned me into a teenager again; in other ways, I was a girl. But sometimes I just felt like a trapped adult woman who was pissed off all the time. This is what's hard to explain, how quickly I could vacillate between being a little girl and being a teenager and being a woman, because of the way they had robbed me of my freedom. There was no way to behave like an adult, since they wouldn't treat me like an adult, so I would regress and act like a little girl; but then my adult self would step back in—only my world didn't allow me to be an adult.

The woman in me was pushed down for a long time. They wanted me to be wild onstage, the way they told me to be, and to be a robot the rest of the time. I felt like I was being deprived of those good secrets of life—those fundamental supposed sins of indulgence and adventure that make us human. They wanted to take away that specialness and keep everything as rote as possible. It was death to my creativity as an artist.

Back in the studio, I made one good song with will.i.am—"Work Bitch." But I wasn't making a lot of music that I was proud of, probably because I wasn't into it. I was so demoralized. It seemed like my father would pick the darkest and ugliest studios to record in. It felt like some people got a thrill from thinking I didn't notice those things. I felt cornered in those situations; I felt they set me up. It was like they thrived on my fear, turned it all into drama, which in turn made me unhappy, and so they would always win. All I knew was I had to work, and I wanted to do the right thing—to make an album that I was proud of. But it was as if I had forgotten that I was a powerful woman.

After *The X Factor*, my manager brought me the offer to perform as part of a Las Vegas residency. I thought, *Why not?*

My heart wasn't in recording music anymore. I wasn't passionately driven, like how I used to be. I had no more fire to bring. I was so over it.

I had two kids. I'd had a breakdown. My parents had taken over my career. What was I going to do at this point, just go home?

So I went along with it.

I went to Vegas the way everyone goes to Vegas—hoping to win.

35

I loved the dry heat of Las Vegas. I loved the way everyone believed in luck and the dream. I had always enjoyed it there, even back when Paris Hilton and I were kicking off our shoes and running through casinos. But that felt like a lifetime ago.

My residency started right after Christmas in 2013. The boys were seven and eight. In the beginning, it was a great gig.

Being onstage in Vegas was thrilling at first. And no one let me forget that my residency was a landmark deal for the Strip. I was told my show drew young people back to Sin City and changed the landscape of entertainment in Las Vegas for a new generation.

The fans gave me so much energy. I became great at doing the show. I got so much confidence, and for a while, everything was good—as good as it could be when I was so tightly controlled. I started dating a TV producer named Charlie Ebersol. To me, he seemed like marriage material: He took great care of himself. His family was close. I loved him.

Charlie worked out every day, taking pre-workout supplements and a whole bunch of vitamins. He shared his nutrition research with me and started giving me energy supplements.

My father didn't like that. He knew what I ate; he even knew when I would go to the bathroom. So when I started taking energy supplements, he saw that I had more energy onstage and that I was in better shape than I had been. It seemed obvious that Charlie's regimens were a good thing for me. But I believe my father started to think that I had a problem with those energy supplements, even though they were over-the-counter, *not* prescription. So he told me I had to get off them, and he sent me to rehab.

He got to say where I went and when. And going to rehab meant that I didn't get to see my kids for a whole month. The only consolation was that I knew it was just for a month and I'd be done.

The place he chose for me was in Malibu. That month, for hours a day, we had to do boxing and other exercises outside, because there was no gym.

A lot of people at the facility were serious drug addicts. I was scared to be there by myself. At least I was allowed to have a security guard, who I'd have lunch with every day.

I found it difficult to accept that my dad was selling himself as this amazing guy and devoted grandfather when he was throwing me away, putting me against my will into a place with crack and heroin addicts. I'll just say it—he was horrible.

When I got out, I started doing shows again in Vegas like nothing had happened. Part of that was because my father told me I had to get back out there, and part of it was because I was still so nice, so eager to please, so desperate to do the right thing and be a good girl.

No matter what I did, my dad was there watching. I couldn't drive a car. Everybody who came to my trailer had to sign waivers. Everything was very, very *safe*—so safe I couldn't breathe.

And no matter how much I dieted and exercised, my father was always telling me I was fat. He put me on a strict diet. The irony was that we had a butler—an extravagance—and I would beg him for real food. "Sir," I would plead, "can you please sneak a hamburger or ice cream to me?"

"Ma'am, I'm sorry," he would say, "I have strict orders from your father."

So for two years, I ate almost nothing but chicken and canned vegetables.

Two years is a long time to not be able to eat what you want, especially when it's your body and your work and your soul making the money that everyone's living off of. Two years of asking for french fries and being told no. I found it so degrading.

A strict diet you've put yourself on is bad enough. But

when someone is depriving you of food you want, that makes it worse. I felt like my body wasn't mine anymore. I would go to the gym and feel so out of my mind with this trainer telling me to do things with my body, I felt cold inside. I felt scared. I'll be honest, I was fucking miserable.

And it didn't even work. The diet had the opposite effect of what my father wanted. I gained weight. Even though I wasn't eating as much, he made me feel so ugly and like I wasn't good enough. Maybe that's because of the power of your thoughts: whatever you think you are, you become. I was so beaten down by all of it that I just surrendered. My mom seemed to go along with my dad's plan for me.

It was always incredible to me that so many people felt so comfortable talking about my body. It had started when I was young. Whether it was strangers in the media or within my own family, people seemed to experience my body as public property: something they could police, control, criticize, or use as a weapon. My body was strong enough to carry two children and agile enough to execute every choreographed move perfectly onstage. And now here I was, having every calorie recorded so people could continue to get rich off my body.

No one else but me seemed to find it outrageous that my father would set all these rules for me and then go out and drink Jack and Cokes. My friends would visit and get their nails done at spas and drink fancy champagne. I was never allowed into spas. My family would stay in Destin, a pretty beach town in Florida, at a ridiculously beautiful condo that I bought for them and eat good-tasting food every night while I was starving and working.

Meanwhile, my sister was turning her nose up at every gift I'd given the family.

I called my mom one day in Louisiana and said, "What are you doing this weekend?"

"Oh, the girls and I are going to Destin tomorrow," she said. Jamie Lynn had said so many times that she never went there, that it was one more of those ridiculous things I'd bought the family that she'd never wanted, and it turned out my mom went there every weekend with Jamie Lynn's two daughters.

I used to love buying my family houses and cars. But there came a point when they started to take things for granted, and the family didn't realize that those things were possible because I'm an artist. And because of how they treated me, for years I lost touch with my creativity.

I was given an allowance of about $2,000 a week. If I wanted a pair of sneakers that my conservators didn't think I needed, I would be told no. This was despite the fact that I did 248 shows and sold more than 900,000 tickets in Vegas. Each show paid hundreds of thousands of dollars.

One of the only nights that I went out with a friend and others, including my dancers, for dinner, I tried to pick up the check for our whole party. The check was a thousand dollars, because the group was so big, but I had wanted to take them out—it was important to me that they knew how much I appreciated how hard they worked. My purchase was declined. I didn't have enough money in my "allowance" account to cover it.

36

One thing that brought me solace and hope during the time when I was in Vegas was teaching dance to kids at a studio once a month, and I loved it. I taught a group of forty kids. Then back in LA, not far from my house, I taught once every two months.

That was one of the most fun things in my life. It was nice to be in a room with kids who had no judgment. In the conservatorship, people were always judging everything I did. The joy and trust of kids the age of the ones I taught—between five and twelve—is contagious. Their energy is so sweet. They want to learn. I find it 100 percent healing to be around children.

One day there, I did a turn and accidentally bonked a tiny little girl in the head with my hand.

"Baby! I am so sorry!" I said.

I felt so bad that I got on my knees in front of her. I pulled a ring off my finger, one of my favorite rings, and gave it to her while begging her forgiveness.

"Miss Britney, it's fine!" she said. "You didn't even hurt me."

I wanted to do anything I could to let her know that I cared if she was in pain and that I would do whatever it took to make it up to her.

Looking up at her from my knees on the dance studio floor, I thought, *Wait a minute. Why are the people who are charged—by the state—with my care not half as interested in my well-being as I am in this little girl's?*

I decided to make a push to get out of the conservatorship. I went to court in 2014 and mentioned my father's alcoholism and erratic behavior, asking that they drug-test him. After all, he was controlling my money and my life. But my case didn't go anywhere. The judge just didn't listen.

What followed was a cloak-and-dagger effort to get my own lawyer. I even mentioned the conservatorship on a talk show in 2016, but somehow, that part of the interview didn't make it to the air. *Huh.* How interesting.

That feeling of being trapped contributed to the collapse of my romantic life. After a stupid fight, Charlie and I got so prideful that we stopped speaking to each other. It was the dumbest thing. I couldn't bring myself to talk to him, and he had too much pride to talk to me.

That's when I started working with two great songwriters, Julia Michaels and Justin Tranter. We'd sit and write everything together. I had passion about it. It was the one thing in the thirteen years of the conservatorship that I really put my heart into. I worked hard on the songs, which gave me confidence. You know when you're good at something and can feel it? You start doing something and think, *I got this?* Writing that album gave me my confidence back.

When it was done, I played it for my sons.

"What should I name the album?" I asked. My kids are really smart about music.

"Just name it *Glory*," Sean Preston said.

And so I did. Seeing the kids so proud of that album meant a lot to me—I thought, *I'm proud of this, too!* It was a feeling I hadn't had in a long time.

I released the video for "Make Me," and I went on the 2016 VMAs to perform in support of it for the first time since 2007.

The first time I saw Hesam Asghari on the set of my video for "Slumber Party," I knew I wanted him in my life immediately.

I was instantly smitten. The chemistry with us in the beginning was insane. We couldn't keep our hands off each other. He called me his lioness.

Right away, the tabloids started to say that he was cheating on me. We'd been dating two weeks! We stayed with each other. I started to feel my spark returning.

Then my dad decided he had to send me to treatment again because I'd snuck my over-the-counter energy supplements. He thought that I had a problem, but he showed mercy and said I could be an outpatient there so long as I'd go four times a week to Alcoholics Anonymous.

At first, I resisted, but the women I met there began to inspire me. I'd listen to them telling their stories and I'd think, *These women are brilliant.* Their stories were actually very, very profound. I found a human connection in those meetings that I'd never found anywhere before in my life. And so at the beginning, I really liked it. But some of the girls didn't always show up. They could pick and choose meetings they wanted to go to. I had no choice in the matter. Friends I met there might only go twice a week, or they'd go to a morning meeting one day and an evening meeting the next day. I wasn't allowed to switch it up at all.

I had the same meetings at the same time every week, no matter what.

* * *

After an exhausting run of shows, I came home, and my sons, my assistant, my mom, and my dad were there.

"Time for your meeting," my dad said.

"Is there a way I can just stay home right now and watch a movie with the boys? I never missed one meeting," I said.

I had never watched a movie with my kids at home in Vegas. I thought we could pop popcorn and have a nice time together.

"No, you have to go," he said.

I looked at my mom, hoping she would stand up for me, but she looked away.

At that moment, I started to feel like I was in a cult and my father was the cult leader. They were treating me like I was beholden to him.

But I was so good, I thought, reflecting on how hard I'd worked in those shows. *I wasn't good, I was great.* It was a line that would run through my mind repeatedly over the next couple years when I thought about the ways in which I had not just met but exceeded the expectations that had been set for me—and how unfair it was that I still wasn't free.

I'd worked so hard and kept up the schedule they set for me—basically four weeks on, four weeks off. When I was on, I did three two-hour shows a week. And on or off, I also kept the weekly schedule they set for me: four AA meetings, two hours of therapy, and three hours of training a week, plus fan meet-and-greets and three shows. I was burned out. And I wanted to control my own destiny.

★　　★　　★

One hairdresser caught a glimpse of my schedule and she said, "Oh, honey, what are you doing?" She had two little girls and was very maternal. I liked her a lot.

"You think it's too much?" I asked her.

"It's more than too much," she said. "That's insane."

She leaned in like she had a secret to tell me. "Listen," she said. "In order to be creative, you have to have room for play in your schedule. It helps ground you to have that time to yourself. Hell, to just stare at the wall if you want. People need that."

It must have gotten back to my father, what she'd said, because the next day, someone else was doing my hair.

I never saw that hairdresser again.

37

As performers, we girls have our hair. That's the real thing guys want to see. They love to see the long hair move. They want you to *thrash* it. If your hair's moving, they can believe you're having a good time.

In the most demoralizing moments of my Las Vegas residency, I wore tight wigs, and I'd dance in a way where I wouldn't move a hair on my head. Everyone who was making money off me wanted me to move my hair, and I knew it—and so I did everything but that.

When I look back, I realize how much of myself I withheld onstage, how much by trying to punish the people who held me captive I punished everyone else, too—including my loyal fans, including myself. But now I know why I'd been sleepwalking through so much of the past thirteen years. I was traumatized.

By holding back onstage, I was trying to rebel in some way, even if I was the only one who knew that was what was happening. And so I didn't toss my hair or flirt. I did the moves and I sang the notes, but I didn't put the fire behind it that I had in the past. Toning down my energy onstage was my own version of a factory slowdown.

As an artist, I didn't feel able to reach the sense of freedom that I'd had before. And that's what we have as artists—that freedom is who we are and what we do. I wasn't free under the conservatorship. I wanted to be a woman in the world. Under the conservatorship, I wasn't able to be a woman at all.

It was different, though, with *Glory*. As the *Glory* singles rolled out, I started getting more passionate about my performances. I started to wear high heels again. When I wasn't trying so hard and I just let myself elevate as a star onstage, that's when it came across the most powerfully. And that's when I could really feel the audiences lifting me up.

Promoting *Glory*, I began to feel better about myself. That third year in Vegas I got a little bit of fire back. I started to appreciate the dazzle of performing in Sin City every night, and the spontaneity of feeling alive in front of an audience. Even though I might not have been doing my best onstage, there were pieces of me that began to awaken again. I was able to tap back into that connection between a performer and an audience.

I have trouble explaining to people who haven't been on-stage what it's like to sense that current between your physical body and the bodies of other human beings in a space. The only metaphor that really works is electricity. You feel *electric*. The energy runs out of you and into the crowd and then back into you in a loop. For such a long time, I'd had to be on auto-pilot: the only current I could access was whatever was inside of me that kept me moving.

Slowly, I began to believe in my capabilities again. For a while I didn't tell anyone. I kept it a secret. Just as I escaped into my dreams to get away from the chaos of my parents when I was a little girl, in Las Vegas, now as an adult but with less freedom than I'd had as a child, I began to escape into a new dream—freedom from my family and a return to being the artist I knew I had in me.

Everything began to seem possible. Hesam and I became so close that we started to talk about having a baby together. But I was in my thirties, so I knew that time was running out.

At the beginning of the conservatorship I was overwhelmed with doctor appointments. Doctor after doctor after doctor—

probably twelve doctors a week—coming to my home. And yet, my father wouldn't let me go to the doctor when I asked for an appointment to get my IUD removed.

When the conservatorship happened, everything became controlled, with security guards everywhere. My whole life changed in a way that might have been safer for me physically but was absolutely horrible for my sense of joy and creativity. A lot of people said, "Oh, your life was saved!" But no, not really. It's the way you look at it. It's perspective. My music was my life, and the conservatorship was deadly for that; it crushed my soul.

Before the conservatorship I'd been in and out of studios recording. During the conservatorship a team of people kept track of when I was going to use the toilet in the recording studio. I'm not even kidding.

I read after the conservatorship that my father and Robin at Lou Taylor's company, Tri Star, had been involved with the security company they hired, Black Box, in monitoring and reviewing calls and texts coming out of and going to my cell phone, including private texts with my boyfriend, my lawyer at the time, and my own kids, and worse, that my father even had a bug put in my home. *In my own home!* This was all part of their control.

I'd left home as a teenager because my family life was so terrible. All those times at four o'clock in the morning when I had to go out into the living room as a little girl and say, "Shut up, Mama!" as my father lay passed-out drunk in his chair—those times would come back to me at four in the morning when I woke up and stared at the ceiling, wondering how those people had come to be in charge again.

In those quiet moments in the middle of the night, I swore to do everything I could to escape.

38

That third year in Vegas, I felt something within me that I hadn't felt in a really, really long time. I felt *strong*. I knew I had to do something.

Once I started to return to myself, my body, my heart, my physicality, and my spiritual self couldn't take the conservatorship any longer. There came a point when my little heart said, *I'm not going to stand for this.*

For so long, my parents had convinced me that I was the bad one, the crazy one, and it worked completely in their favor. It hurt my spirit. They put my fire out. I undervalued myself for a decade. But inside, I was screaming about their bullshit. You have to understand the helplessness in that—the helplessness and the anger.

After my shows, it made me so mad to see my family drinking and having a great time when I wasn't even allowed a sip of Jack and Coke. In the public eye, I know I looked like a star onstage—I had cute tights on and high heels—but why the fuck couldn't I sin in Sin City?

As I became stronger and entered a new phase of my womanhood, I started to look around for examples of how to wield power in a positive way. Reese Witherspoon was a great example to me. She's sweet and she's nice, and she's very smart.

Once you start to see yourself that way—as not just someone who exists to make everyone else happy but someone who deserves to make their wishes known—that changes everything. When I started to think that I could be, like Reese, someone who was nice but also strong, it changed my perspective on who I was.

If no one is used to you being assertive, they get very freaked out when you start speaking your mind. I felt myself turning into their worst fear. I was a queen now, and starting to speak up. I imagined them bowing down to me. I felt my power surging back.

I knew how to carry myself. I'd become strong, enduring that kind of schedule. I really had no choice but to be strong, and I think audiences perceived that. It speaks volumes when you demand respect. It changes everything. And so when I heard my conservators trying to tell me, once again, that I was stupid if I tried to turn down a performance or find a way to give myself some more time off, I felt myself revolt. I thought, *If you guys are trying to trick me into feeling bad for saying no, I'm not going to fall for it again.*

The residency was set to end December 31, 2017. I couldn't wait. For one thing, I was so sick of doing the same show week after week for years. I kept begging for a remix or a new number—*anything* to break up the monotony.

I'd started to lose the joy in performing that I'd felt when I was younger. I no longer had the pure, raw love of singing that I'd had as a teenager. Now other people were telling me what to sing and when. No one seemed to care about what I wanted. The message I kept getting was that their minds mattered; my mind was to be ignored. I was just there to perform for them, to make them money.

It was such a waste. And as a performer who had always taken so much pride in her musicianship, I can't stress enough how mad I was that *they wouldn't even let me change up my show*. We had weeks in between each set of shows in Vegas. So much fucking time was wasted. I wanted to remix my songs for my fans and give them something new and exciting. When I wanted to perform my favorite songs, like "Change Your Mind" or "Get Naked," they wouldn't let me. It felt like they wanted to embarrass me rather than let me give my fans the best possible performance every night, which they deserved. Instead, I had to do the same show week in and week out: the same routines, the same songs, the same arrangements. I'd been doing this same kind of show for a long time. I was desperate to change it up, to give my wonderful, loyal fans a new and electrifying experience. But all I heard was "no."

It was so lazy it was actually odd. I worried about what my fans would think of me. I wished I could communicate that I wanted to give them so much more. I loved to go to studios for hours at a time and do my own remixes with an engineer. But they said, "We can't put remixes in because of the time code of the show. We would have to redo the whole thing." I said, "Redo it!" I'm known for bringing new things to the table, but they always said no.

When I pushed, the best they could offer me, they said, was to play one of my new songs in the background while I was changing.

They acted like they were doing me a huge favor by playing my favorite new song while I was underground frantically taking costumes on and off.

It was embarrassing because I know the business. I knew it was totally possible for us to change up the show. My father was in charge, and it wasn't a priority for him. That meant that the people who would need to make it happen just wouldn't do it. Singing such old versions of songs made my body feel old. I craved new sounds, new movement. I feel now that it might have scared them for me to actually be the star. Instead, my dad was in charge of the star. Me.

When I did the videos for the singles from *Glory*, I felt so light and so free. *Glory* reminded me what it felt like to perform new material and how much I needed it. When I was told I'd be receiving the first-ever Radio Disney Icon Award the year after *Glory* came out, I thought, *This is great! I'll take the boys and wear a cute black dress, and it will be a lot of fun.*

Well, as I sat in the audience seeing a medley of my songs performed, I had so many feelings. By the time Jamie Lynn made a surprise appearance to do a bit of "Till the World Ends" and to hand me my award, I was a ball of emotion.

The whole time I was watching the show, I kept flashing back to the concert special I'd done for *In the Zone*. It was a remixed ABC special. I had rehearsed for a week and sung several new songs. They shot me so beautifully. I felt like a kid. Frankly, it's some of my best work. There was a *Cabaret* vibe to a sultry rendition of ". . . Baby One More Time," and then for "Everytime" I wore a pretty white dress. It was just really, really beautiful. It had felt so incredible to be at that stage of my career, free and performing my music, my way, with so much creative control.

And sitting there to receive the Icon Award at the Radio Disney Music Awards, even while I was honored by the performances, I was furious. Here were three singers and my sister doing new arrangements—something I had begged for, for thirteen years—having fun with my songs in a way I hadn't in hundreds of performances, and I was sitting there having to smile.

39

Before the conservatorship, my friend and agent, Cade, would call me up and say we should go on a road trip, and I'd be in the car before he was done telling me where we were going. If I wanted the volume cranked up at one of my shows, I'd politely make sure the sound guy turned it up. If you pissed me off, everybody would know about it. I was a little badass. But in Vegas I just smiled and nodded and did the same show again and again like a windup doll.

The only thing that kept me going was knowing that I'd have two vacations with my kids, as I did every year. But the year that *Glory* came out, I had to tour instead, which meant I wasn't allowed to go on vacation; I had to take the kids on tour with me, which wasn't fun for anyone. So the following year, I really needed those vacations. One night in the quick-change area before a show, my team came in and I flagged it for them: "Hey," I said, "I just wanted to give you a heads-up. I really need those vacations this year."

Tradition is so important to me. Me and my kids' favorite thing to do was to go to Maui and get a boat and just head out into the ocean. It's for my mental health, honestly.

"If there's a large amount of money," my team said, "we'll go and do, like, two tour shows, and then you can come back and have the whole summer off."

"Great!" I said. "We're on the same page."

A few months went by. Vegas was finally coming to an end in December 2017. I was so relieved. I'd done hundreds of shows.

As I was in my dressing room changing in between acts, someone from my team said, "Hey, yeah, so you are going on tour this year after Vegas ends. We can't just end in Vegas. We have to end it on tour this summer."

"That wasn't the deal," I said. "I told you, I'm taking the kids to Maui."

The conversation escalated quickly, as it usually did when I tried to negotiate. Finally, my team member said: "If you don't go on tour, you will end up in court, because you have a contract." I realized: They were threatening me. And they knew how triggering being in court was for me.

Afterward, I calmed down. I started thinking that if it was just a few weeks, it wouldn't be that bad. Then I could come back and still have something of a summer. We could just go to Maui a little later.

This turned out to be overly optimistic. The tour was hell. I know the dancers felt it, too. We were more locked down than ever by the terms my father set. To even leave the room, we had to give the security team two hours' notice.

To add insult to injury, I was still creatively stifled, still doing the same old thing. They still weren't giving me the freedom to redo my songs and change up the show. We could've changed the show and made something good, something new, that would have felt fresh to the audience and to me and the dancers. That's the only concession I asked for, and again, as always, they said no. Because if I actually took control of my show, it could awaken people to the fact that I might not need my dad as my conservator. I feel like he secretly liked me feeling "less than." It gave him power.

When I finally got home, I cried when I saw my dogs— that's how much I'd missed them. I started to plan a trip to take with the boys to make up for how much time we'd lost. My team said, "We'll give you three weeks off and then we have to start rehearsing for a new Vegas show."

"Three weeks?" I said. "I was supposed to have all summer!" I'd hated the tour.

This felt like being told that the weekend would never come.

40

I could hear the screams already. Hundreds of people had gathered outside. It was an October day in 2018, and there was a huge crowd outside the new Park MGM hotel in Las Vegas. Superfans were dressed in matching clothes and waving flags emblazoned with the letter *B*. Dancers onstage were wearing T-shirts that said BRITNEY. Announcers were livestreaming, hyping up their followers. Laser lights were flashing. A giant screen was showing scenes from my videos. Dance music blasted. A parade went by with marchers loudly singing lyrics like "My loneliness is killing me!"

The lights went down.

Mario Lopez, who was there to host the event, said into the mic, "We are here to welcome the new queen of Vegas . . ."

Dramatic music started—a riff from "Toxic." Crazy lights flashed on the Park MGM so it looked like the building was pulsing. Cue a medley of other songs and projections of a rocket ship, a helicopter, a circus big top, and a snake in the Garden of Eden. Fire blasted up from fire pits around the stage! I rose from the floor on a hydraulic lift, waving and smiling in a tight little black dress with star cutouts and tassels, my hair super long and blond.

". . . Ladies and gentlemen," Mario Lopez continued, "Britney Spears!"

I walked down the stairs in my high heels to "Work Bitch" and signed a few autographs for fans. But then I did something unexpected.

I walked past the cameras.

I kept walking until I got into an SUV and left.

I said nothing. I did not perform. If you were watching, you were probably wondering: *What just happened?*

What you didn't see was that my father and his team were trying to force me to announce the show. I'd said I didn't want to announce it because, as I'd been saying for months, *I didn't want to do it.*

When I'd sung the song "Overprotected" so many years earlier, I'd had no idea what overprotection was. I'd learn soon, because once I made it clear that I wasn't going to keep doing Vegas, my family made me disappear.

41

As the holidays approached, I was feeling pretty good. Aside from my fear that my father was plotting something, I felt strong and inspired by the women I'd met in AA. In addition to being brilliant, they had so much common sense, and I'd learned a lot from them about how to *be* an adult woman navigating the world with honesty and bravery.

For my birthday, Hesam took me somewhere special. I started making holiday plans, but my father insisted that he would be taking the boys for Christmas. If I wanted to see them, I'd have to see my father, too. When I pushed back, my father said, "The boys don't want to be with you this year. They're coming home to Louisiana with me and your mom, and that's that."

"This is news to me," I said, "but if they'd really rather be in Louisiana that week, I guess that's okay."

*   *   *

The Vegas show hadn't been canceled yet. I was hiring new dancers and going over the routines. At a rehearsal one day, I'd been working with all the dancers—both new and old—when one of the dancers who'd been with the show the past four years did a move for us all. I winced when I saw it; it looked really challenging. "I don't want to do that one," I said. "It's too hard."

It didn't seem like a big deal to me, but suddenly my team and the directors disappeared into a room and shut the door. I got the feeling that I had done something horribly wrong, but I didn't understand how not wanting to do one move in a routine could qualify as that. I mean, I was almost five years older than I'd been when the first residency started; my body had changed, too. What difference did it make if we changed it up?

We'd all been having fun, from what I could tell. I have social anxiety, so if there's anything to feel uncomfortable about, I usually feel it first. But that day all seemed well. I was laughing and talking to the dancers. Some of the new ones could do gainers, meaning a standing back tuck going forward. They were amazing! I asked if I could learn it, and one of them offered to spot me on it. All of which is to say: We were playing and communicating. Nothing was going wrong. But the way my team had behaved made me worried something was up.

A day later in therapy, my doctor confronted me.

"We found energy supplements in your purse," he said. The energy supplements gave me a sense of confidence and energy, and you didn't need a prescription for them. He knew that I had been taking them during my shows in Vegas, but now he made a big deal out of it.

"We feel like you're doing way worse things behind our backs," he said. "And we don't feel like you're doing well in rehearsals. You're giving everyone a hard time."

"Is this a joke?" I said.

Instantly, I was furious. I had tried so hard. My work ethic was strong.

"We're going to be sending you to a facility," the therapist said. "And before you go to this place, over Christmas break, we're going to have a woman come to run psychological tests on you."

A flashy doctor—who I'd seen on TV and instinctively hated—came to my house against my will, sat me down, and tested my cognitive abilities for hours.

My father told me that this doctor had concluded that I'd bombed the tests: "She said you failed. Now you have to go to the mental health facility. There's something severely wrong with you. But don't worry—we found you a small rehab program in Beverly Hills. It will only cost you sixty thousand dollars a month."

As I gathered my stuff, crying, I asked how long I should pack for, how long they'd make me stay there. But I was told there was no way to know. "Maybe a month. Maybe two months. Maybe three months. It all depends on how well you do and how well you demonstrate your capabilities." The program was supposedly a "luxury" rehab that had created a special program for me, so I'd be alone and wouldn't have to interact with other people.

"What if I don't go?" I asked.

My father said that if I didn't go, then I'd have to go to court, and I'd be embarrassed. He said, "We will make you look like a fucking idiot, and trust me, you will not win. It's better me telling you to go versus a judge in court telling you."

I felt like it was a form of blackmail and I was being gaslit. I honestly felt they were trying to kill me. I had never stood up to my dad in all those years; I never said no to anyone. My no in that room that day really pissed my dad off.

They forced me to go. They had my back against a wall and I had no choice. *If you don't do this, this is what's going to happen to you, so we suggest you go and get it over with.*

Only that didn't happen—getting it over with, that is. Because once I got there, I couldn't leave, even though I kept begging to.

They kept me locked up against my will for months.

42

The doctors took me away from my kids and my dogs and my house. I couldn't go outside. I couldn't drive a car. I had to give blood weekly. I couldn't take a bath in private. I couldn't shut the door to my room. I was watched, even when I was changing. I had to go to sleep at nine p.m. They supervised me watching TV, from eight to nine o'clock, in bed.

I had to be up every morning at eight. I had endless meetings every day.

For several hours a day, I sat in a chair receiving mandatory therapy. I spent the time in between meetings staring out the window, watching cars pull up and drive away, so many cars bringing so many therapists and security guards, doctors, and nurses. What I think did the most damage to me was watching all those people coming and going while I was prevented from leaving.

I was told that everything that was happening was for my own good. But I felt abandoned in that place, and while everyone kept saying they were there to help me, I never could understand what my family wanted from me. I did everything I was supposed to do. My kids would come for an hour on the weekends. But if I didn't do what I was "supposed to do" during the week, I wouldn't be allowed to see them.

One of the only people who called me was Cade. I've always felt safe and yet also a sense of danger with Cade. The most entertaining call I had the whole time was his FaceTiming me from a hospital in Texas to tell me about how he'd gotten bitten by a scorpion in his bed—*in his bed*. His leg blew up to the size of a basketball, no joke.

"Are you serious right now?" I said, looking at his swollen leg on my phone. It was unbelievably bad. Thinking about Cade's poor leg gave me one of the only true distractions from what I was dealing with, and I'll always be grateful to him and that Texas scorpion.

The therapists questioned me for hours and what seemed like every day, seven days a week.

For years I'd been on Prozac, but in the hospital they took me abruptly off it and put me on lithium, a dangerous drug that I did not want or need and that makes you extremely slow and lethargic. I felt my concept of time morph, and I grew disoriented. On lithium, I didn't know where I was or even who I was sometimes. My brain wasn't working the way it used to. It wasn't lost on me that lithium was the drug my grandmother Jean, who later committed suicide, had been put on in Mandeville.

Meanwhile, my security team that I'd been with for so long acted like I was a criminal.

When it was time for blood draws, the tech drawing my blood would be flanked by the nurse, a security guard, and my assistant.

Was I a cannibal? Was I a bank robber? Was I a wild animal? Why was I treated as though I were about to burn the place down and murder them all?

They checked my blood pressure three times a day, like I was an eighty-year-old woman. And they'd take their time. Make me sit down. Get the cuff. Slowly attach it. Slowly pump it up . . . Three times a day. To feel sane, I needed to move around. Movement was my life as a dancer. I thrived on it. I needed it and craved it. But they kept me in that chair for ages. I began to feel like I was being ritually tortured.

I felt anxious in my feet and in my heart and in my brain. I could never burn off that energy.

You know how when your body is moving you're reminded that you're alive? That's all I wanted. And I couldn't move, which meant I began to wonder if I might actually already be half-dead. I felt *ruined*.

My ass grew bigger from sitting in a chair for hours a day—so much so that none of my shorts fit anymore. I became estranged from my own body. I had terrible nightmares where I was running through a forest—dreams that felt so real. *Please wake up, please wake up, please wake up—I don't want it to be real, this is just a dream*, I would think.

If the idea of my being in that place was to heal, that was not the effect. I began to imagine myself as a bird without wings. You know how, when you're a child, sometimes you run around with your arms outstretched, and with the wind moving over your arms, for a second you feel like you're flying? That was what I wanted to feel. Instead, every day it felt like I was sinking into the earth.

I did the program by myself for two months in Beverly Hills. It was hell, like being in my very own horror movie. I watch scary movies. I've seen *The Conjuring*. I'm not scared of anything after those months at that treatment center. Seriously, I'm not scared of anything now.

I'm probably the least fearful woman alive at this point, but it doesn't make me feel strong; it makes me sad. I shouldn't be this strong. Those months made me too tough. I miss my days of being what in Kentwood we used to call a sass ass. That time in the hospital took away my sassiness. In so many ways, it broke my spirit.

After two months in one building, I was moved to another run by the same people, and at this one I wasn't alone. Even though I used to prefer being by myself, after two months in what felt like solitary confinement and on lithium, it was honestly so much better to be around other patients. We were together all day. At night, each of us was left alone in an individual room—the doors made a *pow* sound as they shut.

My first week, one of the other patients came to my room and said, "Why are you screaming so loud?"

"Huh? I'm not screaming," I said.

"We all hear you. You're screaming so loud."

I looked around my room. "I don't even have music playing," I said.

I later learned that she sometimes heard things other people didn't hear, but that freaked me out.

A very pretty girl arrived and became instantly popular. It felt like high school, where she was the cheerleader and I was the demoralized nerd. She skipped all of the meetings.

Even though a lot of the people there were wild as hell, I liked most of them. One girl smoked thin cigarettes I'd never seen before. She was adorable, and so were her cigarettes. I noticed that her dad would come see her on the weekends. My family, meanwhile, had thrown me into that place and gone about their lives.

"I know you see my cigarettes," the adorable girl said to me one day. "I bet you want to try one, don't you?"

I thought she'd never ask. "Yeah," I said.

And so I smoked my first Capri cigarette with her and some other girls.

A couple of people there had eating disorders and they were distressingly skinny. I didn't eat that much myself. Between how little I was eating and how much blood I was giving for all the tests, I was amazed that I wasn't wasting away.

God must have been with me through that period of time. Three months into my confinement, I started to believe that my little heart, whatever made me Britney, was no longer inside my body anymore. Something bigger must have been carrying me through, because it was too much for me to bear alone.

I look at the fact that I survived and I think, *That wasn't me; that was God.*

43

The hardest part was that I believed that, in front of the doctors or visitors, I had to pretend the whole time I was okay. If I became flustered, it was taken as evidence that I wasn't improving. If I got upset and asserted myself, I was out of control and crazy.

It reminded me of what I'd always heard about the way they'd test to see if someone was a witch in the olden days. They'd throw the woman into a pond. If she floated, she was a witch and would be killed. If she sank, she was innocent, and, oh well. She was dead either way, but I guess they figured it was still good to know what kind of woman she'd been.

After a couple of months, I called my father to beg him to let me go home.

He said, "I'm sorry, the judge is going to have to figure out what she's going to do with you. It's up to the doctors right now. I can't help you at all. I'm giving you to the doctors and I can't help you."

The strange part is, before they put me in that place, my dad had sent me a pearl necklace and a beautiful handwritten card for Christmas. I asked myself, *Why is he doing this? Who is he?*

What hurt me most was that for years he'd been saying in front of the cameras—whether it was when I did the "Work Bitch" video or when the conservatorship first started and we did the Circus Tour—that he was all about me and the boys.

"That's my baby girl!" he'd say right into the camera. "I love her so much." I was stuck in a trailer with Lou's weird-ass lackey Robin, who I'd grown to hate, while he talked about what a great dad he was to anyone who would listen.

But now, when I was refusing to do the new Vegas residency, when I was pushing back on tours, was I still his beloved baby girl?

Apparently not.

A lawyer would later say, "Your dad could've totally put a stop to all that. He could've told the doctors, no, this is too much, let's let my daughter go home." But he didn't.

I called my mom to ask her why everyone was acting like I was so dangerous.

"Well, I don't know, I don't know, I don't know . . ." she would say.

I also texted my sister when I was in that place and asked her to get me out.

"Stop fighting it," she texted back. "There's nothing you can do about it, so stop fighting it."

Along with the rest of them, she kept acting like I was a threat in some way. This will sound crazy, but I'll say it again because it's the truth: I thought they were going to try to kill me.

I didn't understand how Jamie Lynn and our father had developed such a good relationship. She knew I was reaching out to her for help and that he was dogging me. I felt like she should have taken my side.

One of my girlfriends who helped me change clothes every night in the underground changing room during my Vegas run later said, "Britney, I had three or four nightmares when you were at that center. I would wake up in the middle of the night. I had dreams that you killed yourself in that place. And I dreamed that Robin, the lady who was your so-called nice assistant, called me and said proudly, 'Yeah, she died in the place.'" My friend said she worried about me the whole time.

Several weeks into my stay, I was struggling to stay hopeful when one of the nurses, the only one who was real as hell, called me over to her computer.

"Look at this," she said.

I peered at her computer and tried to make sense of what I was seeing. It was women on a talk show talking about me and the conservatorship. One was wearing a #FreeBritney T-shirt.

The nurse showed me clips of other things, too—fans saying they were trying to figure out if I was being held somewhere against my will, talking about how much my music meant to them and how they hated to think I was suffering now. They wanted to help.

And just by doing that, they did help. All the things the nurse was seeing, everyone at the hospital was seeing, too. The doctor eventually noticed that people around the world were asking why I was still locked up. It was all over the news.

The same way I believe that I can sense how someone's feeling in Nebraska, I think my connection to my fans helped them subconsciously know that I was in danger. We have a connection, no matter where we are in space. Even if you're on the other side of the country or the world, on some level we're bound up together. Fans of mine—even though I hadn't said anything online or in the press about being confined—they just seemed to *know*.

Seeing them marching in the streets, chanting "Free Britney!"—that was the most amazing thing I'd ever seen in my life. I know some people laughed at it. They saw the pink T-shirts with my name on them and said, "What kind of cause is this?"

But if they really knew what I was going through and understood the connection I have with my fans, I don't think they would have laughed. The truth is, I was being held against my will. And I did long to know that people might care whether I lived or died.

What do we have except our connections to one another? And what stronger bond is there than music? Everyone who spoke out for me helped me survive that hard year, and the work they did helped me win my freedom.

I don't think people knew how much the #FreeBritney movement meant to me, especially in the beginning. Toward the end, when the court hearings were going on, seeing people advocating for me meant a whole lot. But when it first happened, that got my heart, because I was not okay, not at all. And the fact that my friends and my fans sensed what was happening and did all that for me, that's a debt I can never repay. If you stood up for me when I couldn't stand up for myself: from the bottom of my heart, thank you.

44

When I finally returned to my home and my dogs and my kids, I was ecstatic.

Guess who wanted to come visit me the first week I was back? My family.

"We're so proud of you, Britney!" my dad said. "You did it! Now we all want to come and stay with you." But by this point, I could fully see through his bullshit. I knew what he was really saying was: "I can't wait to see your money—I mean, *you*!"

And so they came—my father, my mom, and my sister, with her daughters, Maddie and Ivey.

I was a shell of myself. I was still on lithium, which made my sense of time really hazy. And I was scared. It crossed my mind that they were only visiting to finish off what they'd started a few months earlier, to kill me for real. If that sounds paranoid, consider all the things I'd been through up until this point—the ways in which they had deceived and institutionalized me.

And so I played the game. *If I'm nice to them, they won't ever try to kill me again*, I thought.

For three and a half months, I'd had barely a hug from anybody.

It makes me want to cry, how strong my little heart had to be.

But my family walked into my house like nothing had happened. Like I hadn't just endured an almost unbearable trauma in that place. "Oh, hey girl, what you doing?" Jamie Lynn said, sounding chipper.

She and my mother and the girls were always hanging around in my kitchen. Jamie Lynn had scheduled all these TV show meetings when she was in Los Angeles. My dad would go with her to the meetings in Hollywood, and she'd come back loud and happy. "What's up, boys?" she'd shout, walking into the kitchen and seeing my sons.

She'd really found her mojo. I was happy for her. At the same time, I didn't particularly want to be around it just then.

"Oh my God, I have this really great idea for me and you!" she'd say after coming back from yet another meeting as I leaned, practically comatose, against the countertop. "Get this—a sister talk show!" Every time she spoke, it was a new scheme. A sitcom! A rom-com!

She talked for what felt like hours at a time while I looked at the floor and listened. And the phrase echoing around my head was *What the fuck is going on?*

Once my family left my house after that terrible visit, I started to really feel what I'd been through. And I was left with nothing but a blind rage. They'd punished me. For what? For supporting them since I was a child?

How had I managed not to kill myself in that place, put myself out of my misery like you'd shoot a lame horse? I believe that almost anyone else in my situation would have.

Thinking about how close I came to doing just that, I wept. Then something happened to knock me out of my stupor.

That August, my father was arguing with Sean Preston, who was thirteen at the time. My son went to lock himself in a bedroom to end the fight, and my dad broke down the door and shook him. Kevin filed a police report, and my father was barred from seeing the kids.

I knew I had to summon one more round of strength, to fight one last time. It had been such a long road. Of finding faith and losing it again. Of being pushed down and getting back up. Of chasing freedom only for it to slip right out of my grasp.

If I was strong enough to survive everything I'd survived, I could take a chance and ask for just a little bit more from God.

I was going to ask, with every bit of my motherfucking blood and skin, for the end of the conservatorship.

Because I didn't want those people running my life anymore. I didn't even want them in my goddamn kitchen.

I didn't want them to have the power to keep me from my children or from my house or from my dogs or from my car ever, ever again.

If I can manifest anything, I thought, *let me manifest an end to this.*

45

The first step toward securing my freedom was for people to begin to understand that I was still a real person—and I knew that I could do that by sharing more of my life on social media. I started trying on new clothes and modeling them on Instagram. I found it incredibly fun. Even though some people online thought it was odd, I didn't care. When you've been sexualized your whole life, it feels good to be in complete control of the wardrobe and the camera.

I tried to get back in touch with my creativity and to follow visual and music artists on Instagram. I came across a guy making trippy videos—one was just a baby-pink screen with a white tiger with pink stripes walking across it. Seeing that, I felt a natural urge to create something myself, and I started playing around with a song. At the beginning of it, I added the sound of a baby laughing. I thought it was different.

Hesam said, "Don't put a baby laughing in it!"

I listened to his advice and took it out, but a while later another account I follow posted a video with a baby laughing, and I was jealous. *I should've done that!* I thought. *That creepy laughing baby should've been* my *thing!*

Artists are weird, you know?

There were so many people in the industry at that time thinking that I was out of my mind. At a certain point, I'd rather be "crazy" and able to make what I want than "a good sport" and doing what everyone tells me to do without being able to actually express myself. And on Instagram, I wanted to show that I existed.

I also found myself laughing more—transported by comedians like Amy Schumer, Kevin Hart, Sebastian Maniscalco, and Jo Koy. I developed such respect for their wit and their cleverness, how they use language to get under people's skin and to make them laugh. That's a gift. Hearing them use their voices—being so distinctively themselves—reminded me that that was something I could do, too, when I made videos on social media or even just in a caption. Humor made it possible for me not to get consumed by bitterness.

I have always admired people in the entertainment industry who have a sharp wit. Laughter is the cure for everything.

People might laugh because things I post are innocent or strange, or because I can get mean when I'm talking about people who've hurt me. Maybe this has been a feminist awakening. I guess what I'm saying is that the mystery of who the real me is, is to my advantage—because nobody knows!

My kids laugh at me sometimes, and when they do it, I don't mind so much.

They've always helped change my perspective on the world. Since they were little, they've always seen things differently, and they're both so creative. Sean Preston is a genius at school—he's really, really bright. Jayden has such an incredible gift with the piano; it gives me chills.

Before the pandemic, they were with me for delicious dinners two or three nights a week. They were always sharing amazing things they'd made and explaining to me what they were excited about.

"Mom, check out this painting I made!" one of them would say. I'd tell them what I saw and they'd say, "Yeah, but now, Mom, look at it like this." And I'd see even more in what they'd made. I love them for their depth and their character, their talent and their goodness.

As we entered a new decade, everything was just starting to make sense again.

Then COVID hit.

For the first months of lockdown, I became even more of a homebody than I already had been. I spent days, weeks, sitting in my room, listening to self-help audiobooks, staring at the wall or making jewelry, bored out of my mind. When I'd run through a ton of self-help audiobooks, I moved on to storytelling ones, anything that turned up under the heading of "Imagination"—especially any book that had a narrator with a British accent.

But out in the world, the security team imposed by my father kept enforcing rules. One day I was on the beach and I took off my mask. Security ran over to scold me. I was reprimanded and grounded for weeks.

Because of the way quarantines were and his work schedule, I didn't have Hesam with me.

I was so lonely, I even got to missing my family.

I called my mom and said, "I want to see you guys."

She said, "We're shopping right now. Gotta go! We'll call you later."

And then they didn't.

The rules of lockdown were different in Louisiana, and they were always out and about.

Eventually, I gave up on getting them on the phone and went to Louisiana to see them. They seemed so free there.

Why did I keep talking to them? I'm not sure. Why do we ever stay in dysfunctional relationships? For one thing, I was still scared of them, and I wanted to make nice. My father still legally was me, as he never hesitated to point out—though I hoped not for long.

It was during this period of time with my family that I

learned that while I'd been in the mental health facility, they'd thrown away a lot of what I'd had stored at my mother's house. The Madame Alexander dolls I'd collected as a girl were all gone. So were three years' worth of my writing. I had a binder full of poetry that had real meaning for me. All gone.

When I saw the empty shelves, I felt an overwhelming sad-ness. I thought of the pages I'd written through tears. I never wanted to publish them or anything like that, but they were important to me. And my family had thrown them in the trash, just like they'd thrown me away.

Then I pulled myself together and I thought: *I can get a new notebook, and I can start over. I've been through a lot. The reason why I'm alive today is because I know joy.*

It was time to find God again.

In that moment, I made peace with my family—by which I mean that I realized I never wanted to see them again, and I was at peace with that.

46

The court-appointed lawyer who had been with me for thirteen years had never been much help, but during the pandemic,
I started to wonder whether maybe I could use him to my advantage. With a prayerlike consistency, I began to speak to him
twice a week, just to meditate on my options. Was he working
for me, or for my father and Lou?

While he talked around the issue, I'd think, *You don't seem to
believe in what I know: I know where I'm going with this. I'm going
all the way to end it. I can tell you're not going to get this done.*

Finally, I hit a turning point. There was honestly no more
that he could do for me. I had to take control.

I had stayed quiet publicly about the whole thing, but I was
praying in my head for it to end. I mean *real* prayer . . .

*   *   *

So on the night of June 22, 2021, from my home in California, I called 911 to report my father for conservatorship abuse.

The time between when I started pushing hard to end the conservatorship and when it finally ended was a rough period in limbo. I didn't know how things would turn out. Meanwhile, I couldn't say no to my dad or make my own way yet, and it felt like every day there was another documentary about me on yet another streaming service. This was what was going on when I learned that my sister would be coming out with a book.

I was still under my father's control. I couldn't say anything to defend myself. I wanted to explode.

Seeing the documentaries about me was rough. I understand that everyone's heart was in the right place, but I was hurt that some old friends spoke to filmmakers without consulting me first. I was shocked that people I'd trusted went on camera. I didn't understand how they could talk about me behind my back like that. If it was me, I would've called my friend to see if it was okay if I talked about her.

There was so much guessing about what I must have thought or felt.

47

"Ms. Spears? You may feel free to address me."

The voice crackled through the phone. I was in my living room. It was an ordinary summer afternoon in Los Angeles.

On June 23, 2021, I was finally due to address a Los Angeles probate court on the subject of the conservatorship. And I knew the world was listening. I had been practicing this for days, but now that the moment was here, the stakes felt overwhelming. Not least because I knew, since I'd asked for this hearing to be open to the public, that millions of people would be listening to my voice as soon as I was done speaking.

My voice. It was everywhere, all over the world—on the radio, on television, on the internet—but there were so many parts of me that had been suppressed. My voice had been used for me, and against me, so many times that I was afraid nobody would recognize it now if I spoke freely. What if they called me crazy? What if they said I was lying? What if I said the wrong thing and it all went sideways? I had written so many versions of this statement. I'd tried a million ways to get it right, to say what I needed to say, but now, in the moment, I was so nervous.

And then, through the fear, I remembered that there were still things I could hold on to: My desire for people to understand what I'd been through. My faith that all this could change. My belief that I had a right to experience joy. My knowledge that I deserved my freedom.

This sense, deeply felt and profound, that the woman in me was still strong enough to fight for what was right.

I looked up at Hesam, who was seated on the couch next to me. He squeezed my hand.

And so, for the first time in what felt like forever, I began to tell my story.

I said to the judge, "I've lied and told the whole world I'm okay and I'm happy. It's a lie. I thought that maybe if I just said that enough, maybe I might become happy, because I've been in denial . . . But now I'm telling you the truth, okay? I'm not happy. I can't sleep. I'm so angry it's insane. And I'm depressed. I cry every day."

I went on to say, "I don't even drink alcohol. I *should* drink alcohol, considering what they put my heart through."

I said, "I wish I could stay with you on the phone forever,

because when I get off the phone with you, all of a sudden all I hear are these nos. And then all of a sudden I feel ganged up on and I feel bullied, and I feel left out, and alone. And I'm tired of feeling alone. I deserve to have the same rights as anybody does, by having a child, a family, any of those things, and more so. And that's all I wanted to say to you. And thank you so much for letting me speak to you today."

I barely breathed. It was the first chance I'd gotten to speak publicly in so long and a million things had come pouring out. I waited to hear how the judge would respond. I hoped I'd get some indication of where her head was at.

"I just want to tell you that I certainly am sensitive to everything that you said and how you're feeling," she said. "I know that it took a lot of courage for you to say everything you have to say today, and I want to let you know that the court does appreciate your coming on the line and sharing how you're feeling."

That made me feel a sense of relief, like I'd finally been listened to after thirteen years.

I have always worked so hard. I put up with being held down for a long time. But when my family put me in that facility, they took it too far.

I was treated like a criminal. And they made me think I deserved that. They made me forget my self-worth and my value.

Of all the things they did, I will say that the worst was to make me question my faith. I never had strict ideas about religion. I just knew there was something bigger than me. Under their control, I stopped believing in God for a while. But then, when it came time to end the conservatorship, I realized one thing: You can't fuck with a woman who knows how to pray. *Really* pray. All I did was pray.

48

I had been lied to for the past thirteen years. The whole world knew I needed a new lawyer, and finally I realized the same thing. It was time to take back control of my own life.

I reached out to my social media team and to my friend Cade for help finding one. This is when I got Mathew Rosengart on board, and he was amazing. A prominent former federal prosecutor now with a major law firm, he had a number of famous clients like Steven Spielberg and Keanu Reeves, and a lot of experience with high-profile, challenging cases. We spoke several times on the phone and then met in early July in my pool house. Once Mathew was in my corner, I felt that I was getting closer to the end. Something had to happen. It couldn't stay at a standstill. But of course, because it was the legal system, we had to do a lot of waiting and strategizing.

He was appalled that I'd been denied my own lawyer for

so long. He said even vicious criminals get to pick their own lawyers, and he said he hated bullying. I was glad, because I saw my father and Lou and Robin as bullies and I wanted them out of my life.

Mathew said he would go to court and file a motion to remove my dad as conservator first, and then, after that, it would be easier to try to terminate the entire conservatorship. Just a few weeks later, on July 26, he filed to eliminate my father from that role. After a big court hearing on September 29, my father was suspended as my conservator. It was all over the news before Mathew could even call me after court.

I felt relief sweep over me. The man who had scared me as a child and ruled over me as an adult, who had done more than anyone to undermine my self-confidence, was no longer in control of my life.

At that point, with my father eliminated, Mathew told me we had momentum, and he petitioned for the end of the conservatorship altogether.

I was at a resort in Tahiti in November when Mathew called me with the news that I was no longer under a conservatorship. He'd told me when I left for the trip that one day soon I'd be able to wake up for the first time in thirteen years a free woman. Still, I couldn't believe it when he called me as soon as he came out of the court hearing and told me it was done. I was free.

Even though it was his strategy that had gotten us the victory, he told me that I deserved the credit for what had happened. He said that by giving my testimony, I'd freed myself and probably also helped other people in unfair conservatorships. After having my father take credit for everything I did for so long, it meant everything to have this man tell me that I'd made the difference in my own life.

And now, finally, it *was* my own life.

Being controlled made me so angry on behalf of anyone who doesn't have the right to determine their own fate.

"I'm just grateful, honestly, for each day . . . I'm not here to be a victim," I said on Instagram after the conservatorship was terminated. "I lived with victims my whole life as a child. That's why I got out of my house. And worked for twenty years and worked my ass off . . . Hopefully, my story will make an impact and make some changes in the corrupt system."

In the months since that phone call, I've been trying to rebuild my life day by day. I'm trying to learn how to take care of myself, and to have some fun, too.

On vacation in Cancún, I got to do something I'd loved years earlier—Jet Skiing. The last time I'd Jet Skied before that had been in Miami with the boys, when I went too fast because I was trying to keep up with them. Those kids are borderline dangerous on a Jet Ski! They go extremely fast and do jumps. Riding over the waves after them, I was hitting hard—*boom, boom, boom*—and falling down, wiping out and hurting my arm.

Not wanting to repeat that experience, in May 2022 I got my assistant to drive me instead. It's way better when someone drives you, I've found. This time I could feel the power of the engine, I could enjoy being out on the clear blue water, and I could go exactly the speed I wanted to.

That's the kind of thing I'm doing now—trying to have fun and trying to be kind to myself, to take things at my own pace. And, for the first time in a long time, allowing myself to trust again.

Every day, I put music on. When I walk around my house singing, I feel completely free, completely at ease, completely happy. Whether I sound perfect or not, I don't even care. Singing makes me feel confident and strong the same way exercise does, or prayer. (Remember: your tongue is your sword.) Anything that gets your heart rate up is good. Music is that, plus a connection to God. That's where my heart is.

When I had full-time access to a studio in Malibu, I loved going there regularly. One day I created six songs. Music is at its purest for me when I'm doing it for myself. I thought I might get a studio again someday and just play around, but for some time I hadn't been thinking about recording.

I changed my mind about that when I got invited to record a song with an artist I've admired my entire life: Sir Elton John. He's one of my all-time favorite performers. I'd met him at an

Oscars party about a decade ago and we got along so well. And now here he was reaching out with the sweetest video message, asking if I would be interested in collaborating on one of his most iconic songs. "Hold Me Closer" would be a modernized duet version of his hit "Tiny Dancer," with bits of a couple of his other songs, too.

I was so honored. Like me, Elton John has been through so much, so publicly. It's given him incredible compassion. What a beautiful man on all levels.

To make the collaboration even more meaningful: as a child, I listened to "Tiny Dancer" in the car in Louisiana as I rode to and from my dance and gymnastics classes.

Sir Elton was kind and made me feel so comfortable. Once we'd worked out a date to record the song, I headed over to the producer's home studio in Beverly Hills.

The studio was in the basement of the house. I had never seen a setup like it: it was a completely open studio with guitars, pianos, soundboards, and music equipment all set out. I was nervous because it would be the first time the world had heard my singing voice on something new in six years, but I believed in the song and in myself, so I went for it.

I stood in front of the microphone, sped up the tempo, and began to sing. After a few hours, we were done. I had recorded a duet with one of my favorite artists on one of my favorite songs. I was excited, anxious, and emotional in the weeks leading up to the release.

Before the conservatorship, I would go onstage and every-one would look to me for the signal that it was time to start the show. I'd hold up my index finger to say, "Let's go." Under the conservatorship, I always had to wait for everyone else. I was told, "We'll let you know when we're ready." I didn't feel like they treated me as if I had any value. I hated it.

I'd been taught through the conservatorship to feel almost too fragile, too scared. That's the price I paid under the conservatorship. They took a lot of my womanhood, my sword, my core, my voice, the ability to say "Fuck you." And I know that sounds bad, but there is something crucial about this. Don't underestimate your power.

"Hold Me Closer" debuted on August 26, 2022. By August 27, we were number one in forty countries. My first number one and my longest-charting single in almost ten years. And on my own terms. Fully in control. Fans said that on the track I sounded amazing. Sharing your work with the world is terrifying. But in my experience, it is always worth-while. Recording "Hold Me Closer" and putting it out into the world was a fantastic experience. It didn't feel good—it felt *great*.

Pushing forward in my music career is not my focus at the moment. Right now it's time for me to try to get my spiritual life in order, to pay attention to the little things, to slow down.

It's time for me not to be someone who other people want; it's time to actually find myself.

As I've gotten older, I like my alone time. Being an entertainer was great, but over the last five years my passion to entertain in front of a live audience has lessened. I do it for myself now. I feel God more when I'm alone.

I'm no saint, but I do know God.

I have a lot of soul-searching to do. It's going to be a process. I'm already enjoying it. Change is good. Hesam and I always pray together. I look up to him—his consistency with working out and being a good man and being healthy and taking care of me and helping me learn how we can take care of each other.

He's such an inspiration and I'm grateful. The timing of the end of the conservatorship was perfect for our relationship; we were able to establish a new life together, without limitations, and get married. Our wedding was a beautiful celebration of how much we'd been through together and how deeply we wished for each other's happiness.

The day the conservatorship ended, I was left with so many emotions: shock, relief, elation, sadness, joy.

I felt betrayed by my father and, sadly, by the rest of my family, too. My sister and I should have found comfort in each other, but unfortunately that hasn't been the case. As I was fighting the conservatorship and receiving a lot of press atten-tion, she was writing a book capitalizing on it. She rushed out salacious stories about me, many of them hurtful and outra-geous. I was really let down.

Shouldn't sisters be able to confess their fear or vulner-ability to each other without that later being used as evidence of instability?

I couldn't help but feel that she wasn't aware of what I'd been through. It appeared that she thought it had been easy for me because so much fame had come to me so young, and that she blamed me for my success and everything that came with it.

Jamie Lynn clearly suffered in our family home, too. She grew up a child of divorce, which I did not. It seems that she didn't get a lot of parenting, and I know it was hard to try to sing and act and make her own way in the world in the shadow of a sibling who got not only most of the family's attention but a lot of the world's. My heart goes out to her for all those reasons.

But I don't think she fully understands just how desper-ately poor we were before she was born. Because of the money I brought to the family, she wasn't helpless in the face of our father, like my mother and I were back in the 1980s. When you have nothing, that pain gets intensified by your inability to escape. My mom and I had to witness the ugliness and the violence without believing that there was anywhere else to go.

She will always be my sister, and I love her and her beautiful family. I wish the absolute best for them. She's been through a lot, including teen pregnancy, divorce, and her daughter's near-fatal accident. She's spoken about the pain of growing up in my shadow. I'm working to feel more compassion than anger toward her and toward everyone who I feel has wronged me. It's not easy.

I've had dreams in which June tells me he knows he hurt my father, who then hurt me. I felt his love and that he'd changed on the other side. I hope that one day I will be able to feel better about the rest of my family, too.

My anger has been manifesting itself physically, especially with migraine headaches.

When I get them, I don't want to go to the doctor because being sent to one doctor after another all those years gave me a phobia about them. And so I take care of things myself. When it comes to the migraines, I don't like to talk about them because I'm superstitious that if I do, they'll bother me more.

When I have one, I can't go into the light and I can't move. I stay very still in the dark. Any light makes my head throb and makes me feel like I'm going to pass out—it's that painful. I have to sleep for a day and a half. Until recently, I'd never had a headache in my whole life. My brother used to complain about his headaches and I thought he was exaggerating how bad they were. Now I'm sorry I ever said anything to doubt him.

For me, a migraine is worse than a stomach virus. At least with a bug you can still think straight. Your head can help you figure out what you want to do, what movies you want to watch. But when you have a migraine you can't do anything because your brain is gone. Migraines are just one part of the physical and emotional damage I have now that I'm out of the conservatorship. I don't think my family understands the real damage that they did.

For thirteen years, I wasn't allowed to eat what I wanted, to drive, to spend my money how I wanted, to drink alcohol or even coffee.

Freedom to do what I want to do has given me back my womanhood. In my forties, I'm trying things for what feels like the first time. I feel like the woman in me was pushed down for so long.

Now, finally, I'm roaring back to life. I might actually be able to go sin in Sin City, too.

49

I've started to experience the riches of being an adult woman for the first time in many years. I feel like I've been underwater for so long, only rarely swimming up to the surface to gasp for air and a little food. When I regained my freedom, that was my cue to step out onto dry land—and, any time I want, to take vacations, sip a cocktail, drive my car, go to a resort, or stare out at the ocean.

I've been taking it a day at a time and trying to be thankful for the little things. I'm thankful that my father is not in my life. I don't have to be scared of him anymore. If I gain weight, it's a relief to know that no one is going to be there shouting at me, "You need to pick it up!" I get to eat chocolate again.

As soon as my father was no longer around, making me eat what he wanted me to eat, my body became strong and my fire came back. I had confidence, and I started to like how I looked again. I love playing dress-up on Instagram.

I know that a lot of people don't understand why I love taking pictures of myself naked or in new dresses. But I think if they'd been photographed by other people thousands of times, prodded and posed for other people's approval, they'd understand that I get a lot of joy from posing the way I feel sexy and taking my own picture, doing whatever I want with it. I was born into this world naked, and I honestly feel like the weight of the world has been on my shoulders. I wanted to see myself lighter and freer. As a baby, I had my whole life in front of me, and that's how I feel now, like a blank slate.

I really do feel reborn. Singing as I walk around at home just like I did as a little girl, I enjoy that feeling of the sound leaving my body and bouncing back at me. I'm finding the joy again of why I wanted to sing to begin with. That feeling is sacred for me. I do it for me and for nobody else.

I keep getting asked when I'm going to put on shows again. I confess that I'm struggling with that question. I'm enjoying dancing and singing the way I used to when I was younger and not trying to do it for my family's benefit, not trying to get something, but doing it for me and for my genuine love of it.

Only now do I feel like I'm getting back my trust in other people and my faith in God. I know what makes me happy and brings me joy. I try to meditate on those places and thoughts that enable me to experience it. I love beautiful places, my sons, my husband, my friends, my pets. I love my fans.

When it comes to fans, people sometimes ask me about my special relationship with the gay community.

For me, it's all about love—unconditional love. My gay friends were always protective of me, maybe because they knew that I was kind of innocent. Not dumb, but way too kind. And I think a lot of the gay guys around me took on a supportive role. I could even feel it onstage when they were beside me. If I thought I didn't do my best performance, I could count on my friends to realize I didn't feel great about it and still say, "You did so good!" That kind of love means everything to me.

Some of my favorite nights were when I would go out with my dancers. One time in Europe we went to a gay club where I felt like everyone around me on the dance floor was *so tall*. The club played great electro dance music and I loved it. I danced until six o'clock in the morning and felt like it went by in two seconds. My heart was so alive. It was like the mystical time in Arizona—it was a spiritual experience to be with people who I could feel loved me unconditionally. With friends like that, it doesn't matter what you do or say or who you know. That's true love.

I remember one time in Italy, too, I went to a showcase where some drag artists were doing my songs. It was so amazing. The artists were beautiful. They were living in the moment and I could tell they loved to perform. They had such heart and drive, and I respect that a lot.

Once I was freed from the conservatorship, I got to go to the two vacation places that I'd missed, Maui and Cancún. I swam in the ocean; sat out in the sun; played with my new puppy, Sawyer; and took boat rides with Hesam. I read a lot and I wrote this book. While I was traveling, I found out that I was pregnant. I'd wanted another baby for so many years. For a long time, Hesam and I had been eager to start our own family. I have an appreciation for how stable he is. I love that he doesn't even drink. He's a gift from God. And to find out that he and I were about to have a child together made me feel giddy.

I was also scared. When I was pregnant with Sean Preston and Jayden, I suffered from depression. Pregnancy this time felt the same in a lot of ways—I felt a little sick and loved food and sex—and so I wondered if the depression would return, too. I did feel a little bit slower. I like to be up and with it. But my life was so much better and I had so much support that I felt confident I could make it through.

Before the end of my first trimester, I miscarried. I'd been so thrilled to be pregnant that I'd told the whole world, which meant I had to un-tell them. We posted on Instagram: "It is with our deepest sadness we have to announce that we have lost our miracle baby early in the pregnancy. This is a devastating time for any parent. Perhaps we should have waited to announce until we were further along. However, we were overly excited to share the good news. Our love for each other is our strength. We will continue trying to expand our beautiful family. We are grateful for all of your support. We kindly ask for privacy during this difficult moment."

I was devastated to have lost the baby. Once again, though, I used music to help me gain insight and perspective. Every song I sing or dance to lets me tell a different story and gives me a new way to escape. Listening to music on my phone helps me cope with the anger and sadness I face as an adult.

I try not to think too much about my family these days, but I do wonder what they will think of this book. Because I was silenced for thirteen years, I wonder if, when they see me speaking out, they've had the occasional thought, *Maybe she's right*. I believe they have a guilty conscience, that they know deep down that it was very, very wrong to do to me what they did.

From all those years making myself do what I was told and being treated in a certain way, I've come to see what kind of people I want to be around and what kind of people I don't. So much of the media was cruel to me, and that hasn't changed just because I am out of the conservatorship. There's been a lot of speculation about how I'm doing. I know my fans care. I am free now. I'm just being myself and trying to heal. I finally get to do what I want, when I want. And I don't take a minute of it for granted.

Freedom means being goofy, silly, and having fun on social media. Freedom means taking a break from Instagram without people calling 911. Freedom means being able to make mistakes, and learning from them. Freedom means I don't have to perform for anyone—onstage or offstage. Freedom means that I get to be as beautifully imperfect as everyone else. And freedom means the ability, and the right, to search for joy, in my own way, on my own terms.

It took a long time and a lot of work for me to feel ready to tell my story. I hope it inspires people on some level and can touch hearts. Since I've been free, I've had to construct a whole different identity. I've had to say, *Wait a second, this is who I was—someone passive and pleasing. A girl. And this is who I am now—someone strong and confident. A woman.*

When I was a little girl lying on the warm rocks in my neighbors' garden, I had big dreams. I felt calm and in control. I knew I could make my dreams come true. For so long, I didn't always have the power to make the world look the way I wanted it to, but in many ways I do now. I can't change the past, but I don't have to be lonely or scared anymore. I've been through so much since I wandered the Louisiana woods as a child. I've made music, traveled all over the world, become a mother, found love and lost it and found it again. It's been a while since I felt truly present in my own life, in my own power, in my womanhood. But I'm here now.

ACKNOWLEDGMENTS

If you follow me on Instagram, you thought this book was going to be written in emojis, didn't you? 🌷 🌷 🌷 🌷 🌷 🌷

Thank you to the team who worked so hard to help me bring my memoir into the world, including: Cade Hudson; Mathew Rosengart; Cait Hoyt; my collaborators (you know who you are); and Jennifer Bergstrom, Lauren Spiegel, and everyone at Gallery Books.

Thank you to my fans: You have my heart and my gratitude forever. This book is for you.

ABOUT THE AUTHOR

Multi-platinum, Grammy Award-winning pop icon Britney Spears is one of the most successful and celebrated entertainers in music history, with more than 100 million records sold worldwide. In 2021, she was named one of *Time* magazine's 100 Most Influential People. Spears's album *Blackout* was added to the Rock & Roll Hall of Fame's Library & Archives in 2012. She lives in Los Angeles, California.